D0742326

Grumpy Old Drivers

Stuart Prebble

Illustrations by Noel Ford

For my brother, Steve.

Weidenfeld & Nicolson
London

First published in Great Britain in 2008
by Weidenfeld & Nicolson

10 9 8 7 6 5 4 3 2 1

Text © Stuart Prebble 2008
Illustrations © Noel Ford 2008

A CIP catalogue record for this book is available from the British Library.

ISBN: 978 0 297 85433 3

Printed and bound in Great Britain by Mackays of Chatham plc, Chatham, Kent

Weidenfeld & Nicolson
The Orion Publishing Group Ltd
Orion House, 5 Upper Saint Martin's Lane, London WC2H 9EA
www.orionbooks.co.uk

An Hachette Livre UK Company

The Orion Publishing Group's policy is to use papers that are natural, renewable and recy-
clable products and made from wood grown in sustainable forests. The logging and manu-
facturing processes are expected to conform to the environmental regulations of the
country of origin.

Contents

Acknowledgements

Thanks to the whole team at Liberty Bell Productions who make commuting just about worth doing. Also to everyone at Orion, especially Alan Samson, Lucinda McNeile and Rosie Anderson. Roly Keating, Elaine Bedell and Gilly Hall at the BBC. Marilyn and Alex, of course. And especially all the arsehole drivers who unknowingly provided so much material for this volume.

Introduction

I know, I know, we've cried wolf before.

In the past we've said that automated call centres are the worst thing.

We've said that Christmas is the worst thing.

We've said that working for wankers is the worst thing.

We've said that holidays are the worst thing. New Year. Kids. Relationships. Lift music. Call centres. John McCrirrick …

But actually it's driving. No, really, it is. It's driving.

Driving is the worst thing of all because it brings together so many of the multitude of individual elements which combine to make Grumpy Old Men and Grumpy Old Women grumpy. Just think about it for a minute. It's got the lot.

It's got queuing – at petrol stations, on side roads, on A-roads, on slip-roads, on motorways, at car parks, for ferries, and even at the 'drive through'. Very few things make Grumpies more grumpy than queuing.

It's got being ripped off – when you buy it, when you have it serviced, when you buy anything for it, when anything goes

DISAPPOINTMENT
OVER
EXPECTATION
AHEAD

wrong, when you put petrol in it, when you wash it, when you park it, when it gets towed away and when some arsehole you've never met bumps into it. Yes, we Grumpies hate being ripped off.

It's got being pissed about – again, when you buy it, when you want to book it in for a service, and when you get to tax it, insure it and get the MOT for it, when it gets ticketed or towed away, and again when you want to sell it. Driving has an entire arsenal of ways to have us pissed about, and Grumpies are positively allergic to being pissed about.

And last but not least, it's got that most essential ingredient of our Grumpiness: driving is a triumph of disappointment over expectation. When we were kids we thought driving would be wonderful, the ultimate freedom, the keys to the highway, and all it has turned out to be is a total and colossal pain in the tushkin.

And all that is not to mention *Top* fucking *Gear*.

So driving. That's what this book is about. And sure, sure, plenty has already been written about driving. God knows there is a supplement in practically every weekend newspaper, there are countless magazines, books, reviews, endless websites, and loads of TV programmes – I believe that until fairly recently even an entire channel called *Men and Motors*. However, none of them, I do assure you, has looked at driving from quite our perspective.

No, not quite our perspective.

1 'Where do you bloody well start ... ?'

I live in Kingston upon Thames, just about a mile up the hill from Kingston Hospital. You probably don't know it, but Kingston Hospital is a busy general hospital with a large accident and emergency department serving a very wide surrounding area. Not unlike the general hospital somewhere near you, I daresay.

So one of the things you would probably expect about a hospital with a busy accident and emergency department is that there will be quite a few ambulances coming and going, at all hours of the day and night. And one of the things that we know about ambulances is that they are quite often in a bit of a hurry. Indeed, when they are in a bit of a hurry, it's not infrequently a matter of life and death. I'm not talking about the usual irritating but essentially trivial old bollocks that most of us choose to exaggerate about. I mean the real thing.

Indeed, inside any one of those big white vehicles with a red cross on the side it could easily be you, or it could easily be me, or it could easily be someone that you or I love or care about. So important stuff then. We all take it seriously.

Mostly when we hear one coming up behind us we go to some trouble to veer out of the way (of which more later). We want to let the ambulance speed by. At some level, we all have a sense of 'there but for the grace of God go I', and we don't want to be the person responsible for holding up the mission of mercy for just that vital few seconds which could be the difference between miracle and tragedy.

So right then. If, by any accident of chance or happenstance, you found yourself responsible for the road system or the management of traffic around the area of this or any other hospital, I wonder what would be among your priorities? We're assuming, just for the sake of this little exercise, that you have more than one brain cell, which you aren't sharing between 15 or 20 other people, and that you don't have a specific agenda born out of sadism or general misanthropy.

Yes, you got there. One of the things you would regard as a priority in the roads leading to and from a general hospital is *that the ambulances could get in and out. Quickly!*

What then, would you imagine, have the people responsible for planning the roads around Kingston Hospital done? How have they responded, do you suppose, to this little facet of everyday life, this self-evidently basic requirement arising from loads of people all living close together in a communal space? Go on, you can play this one at home. See if you can guess.

Well, the answer is of course that the highways agency, or the local council, or the traffic management wonks, or whoever they are, have taken this opportunity to have enormous fun. No no, on reflection that doesn't quite state it. Doesn't quite do justice to it. It's more than that. More than fun, they've taken this as an invitation to have an absolute bloody field day. The equivalent of the works outing, the annual paint-balling jaunt or trip to Alton Towers.

These bloody people have delved into the thick and comprehensive catalogue from which they presumably usually choose their Christmas presents, and have come up with a unique medley of stationary obelisks, speed bumps, road signs, road narrowing and road blocks. Yes, these excellent public servants, every one of them in the pay of you and me, have selected this particular little area to install the widest possible selection from their arsenal of resources designed to make life more difficult for the rest of us. Oh yes, they have really managed to get their rocks off.

All along Gloucester Road, a main route for traffic coming to and from Kingston Hospital, there has been installed a positive commando course of strategically placed speed bumps. Some in pairs on either side of the road, and some singles smack in the middle of the road. Whether in singles or in pairs, these obstacles have undoubtedly been designed to force drivers to select from among three options.

Option one, you can choose to steer the car so that you bump over these mounds in the road with two wheels, which has the effect of raising one side of the vehicle so high that there is an imminent risk of cracking your head on the car roof. Not an attractive choice, this, but it does at least have the virtue of keeping you on your side of the road, and therefore minimising the risk of collision with an oncoming vehicle. That's option one.

Option two is that you can try to manoeuvre the car so that the wheels fall on the edges of the obstacles. Helpfully the bumps are just a bit wider than the gap between the wheels on the left side of your car and the wheels on the right side of your car, so there is no chance that you can get away without any bump whatever, but at least you can minimise the impact. However, the downside is that this course of action involves swerving violently into the middle of the road, and directly into the path of any approaching cars.

Option three is that you can slow down to the speed of a one-legged penguin trying to cross the Gobi desert, edge over the speed bumps, and only thereby avoid significant damage to self or car or other occupants.

There is no fourth alternative.

However, obviously the installation of half a dozen speed bumps in the course of a few hundred yards may not cause quite enough inconvenience and bloody stupidity to satisfy these aforementioned wonks. No, not nearly enough. So, from time to time along this same route to and from the hospital with the A & E department, the geniuses responsible for this little area have widened the pavement on both sides, leaving just one lane open on the existing carriageway. This has the effect of causing traffic coming from both directions to play a continuous game of Mexican stand-off, as everyone tries to determine whether you were approaching the road narrows first, and therefore have the right of way, or they were approaching the road narrows first and have the right of way.

Frequently it is by no means clear, and there is no 'give way to oncoming traffic' sign facing either direction, so this in turn means that everyone gets irritated at everyone else, and everybody mouths or shouts 'bastard' at anyone who barrels through, or who doesn't acknowledge the fact that you have waited. In either eventuality, the overall effect is a further delay for all concerned. Good job the A & E department is handy.

If you didn't know anything about what motivates the particular arse-heads we are talking about – about what makes them get up in the morning and jog to work with that special spring in their step – you might easily think that a combination of road narrows and sleeping policemen would be enough fun for one day. This would be an important misunderstanding. These chaps have by no means finished yet. Because, extraordinarily, this road is one of the few already narrow roads locally in which residents are allowed to park their cars on both sides of the road.

What this in turn means is that, more often than not, there is nowhere for the driver who has decided or been obliged to wait for the oncoming car to come through, to pull out of the way of oncoming traffic. Are you getting this? Sound familiar?

All this has the result that a thoroughfare which would anyway be constantly busy simply due to the weight of traffic, but which could at least have free-flowing lanes in both directions, has intermittent hold-ups all the way along the route, day and night, night and day.

And this, to remind ourselves, is on one of the major routes taken by ambulances, or indeed any other vehicle which may need to get to the casualty department on a matter of life and death. Any vehicle approaching the hospital from this direction has to swerve, and stop, and indicate, and wait, and crash their suspension, and wait some more. And since a proportion of the emergency cases in the back of ambulances are likely to involve spinal injuries, the inevitable bump delivered into the vehicle as a result of negotiating this series of speed bumps, must frequently cause pain and suffering. Pain and suffering, which are even more excruciating than those suffered routinely by Grumpy Old Men such as ourselves when travelling up and down this road, and the tens of thousands of other roads like it, the length and breadth of the country.

All of which is not to mention the deaths or irretrievably worsened conditions that must have been caused by the additional delays which are the result of these so-called 'traffic-calming' measures. Traffic calming. Is that the effect it has on you? Calming? Calming? All I want to do is to reach for the twelve bore.

So here is the thing, and this is obvious to me, and it's obvious to you, and it's obvious to every rational person in the country who doesn't have some sort of vested interest in making all of our lives more difficult. By all means, if these bastards want to, impose speed restrictions. By all means, if they must, install ever more sodding cameras designed to monitor our every move and fart and incident of aggravated nose-picking from the moment we open our eyes in the morning to the moment we close them at night. By all means increase the penalties, if they must, for reckless driving, or careless driving, or driving while thinking about which of Pan's People we most would have liked to have slept with.

But don't put sodding obstacles in the road! Geddit? Sometimes – not very often, thank God – but sometimes we may all have occasion to need to speed to hospital when there is an emergency. Or maybe sometimes we won't have a good reason, but our attention has wandered, or there is a thick fog, or maybe something has happened which makes haste unavoidable. In such circumstances, the potential consequences of excess speed are bad enough without some dumb, stupid, malevolent ignoramus putting a bloody great piece of kerb right in the middle of the carriageway.

If it's a sleeping policeman, it threatens to put our heads through the roof of the car. If it's a bit of extended pavement it threatens to put our heads through the windscreen. So don't do it. Huh?

What all this brings us back to is this – and here we are in familiar Grumpy territory – the world is divided into two categories. One category contains those of us who are trying our best to live our lives, do a decent day's work, earn a reasonable living, pay the mortgage, feed the family, have an occasional holiday, go out for the odd visit to the cinema or meal. The other category is the people who are trying to mess us up. In this second category are the people who spend some or all of every day sitting around thinking about new ways to make our lives a bit more difficult.

These chaps turn up to work in the morning, have a cup of tea, scratch their privates, and then reach for a plan of a road lay-out somewhere in the neighbourhood which may be working reasonably well, and consider what options are available to them to make it all a bit more difficult.

How much inconvenience would it cause, for example, if we were to make this a 'no right turn'? Yes, tempting; people have been turning right here for a hundred years, and seem to have been causing no problem to anyone, so perhaps a 'no right turn' might be quite appropriate. On the other hand, since not all that many people want to turn right, what about introducing a filter light so that the rest of the drivers who don't want to turn right have to sit waiting even longer while no-one turns right on the green arrow? Yes, it has its merits. Or we could just further extend the time when everyone is waiting on the red light and no-one is crossing the road. Or indeed we could widen the traffic island. Or put some new railings around the traffic island. Or change the speed limit every three hundred yards or so, with the effect that drivers of cars will feel like the shiny metal ball in a pinball machine, being bounced and buffeted and re-directed and abruptly stopped, all on their journey to eventually falling down the drain. Or change the texture of the pavement so that the partially sighted, who never use this junction but one day might, can feel underfoot that they are coming to the end of the kerb. Or we can put in a ramp because, although no wheel-chair user has used this crossing for a decade, who knows, one day one might.

Dozens of options, and hundreds and thousands of junctions and crossroads and corners and bends and roundabouts to choose from. An endless range of opportunities, all of them promising new chances to create mayhem for each and every one of us from now 'til retirement and beyond. And all that public money to spend! All those drivers sitting, waiting even longer while the work is being carried out, and longer still once it has been completed. Oh joy. Oh bliss.

And it's not as though these people are doing this unbidden. Not as though some unseen enemy is paying them to make our lives tougher day by day. We're paying them ourselves! Each and every one of us sits in our cars, day after day, head in hands, fingers drumming on the steering wheel, quietly losing our minds and contemplating the routine idiocy that these people perpetrate – at our expense.

Does anyone see the sense of it? Can anyone understand why on earth we would put up with it? Why we don't rise up, as one, and say 'we're as mad as hell, and we ain't going to take it any more'? Does anyone get it? I'm perfectly sure that I bloody don't.

And the ambulances trying to get to Kingston Hospital? Well as a rule, Grumpy Old Men and Grumpy Old Women try not to wish actual harm to other people. It's not good for the soul. Not good for the karma. But which of us has not fantasised about one of the twots who has dreamed up this jerk-off idea suffering a minor but extremely painful back injury, and being carried in an ambulance over the very bumps and obstacles which he has caused to be installed? And which of us has not envisioned the resulting increased agony, or extended delay in receiving palliative treatment?

Or is that just me?

2 From the word 'go'

There is no individual area of our lives where the contrast between the expectation and the delivery is so great.

I know. I acknowledged earlier that it's a big claim. God knows there are enough areas where as kids we Grumpies thought life was going to be wonderful and it has turned out to be shit, but I genuinely believe that we're going to be able to justify this lofty statement for the whole business of driving.

I think that for boys in particular it is part of our DNA. We are preoccupied with cars and driving them from the word go. That's probably why the word 'go' is the word 'go'. As kids we always just want to 'go' and cars were what our 'going' dreams were made of.

Just about ten seconds after we can say 'mumma' or whatever, boys are charging about the place and making the noise of screaming tyres as they go around corners, arms contorting as they grapple with the virtual steering wheel, just barely coping with the centrifugal force produced by swerving, and adjusting their voice boxes to differentiate the squealing sounds of going around a sharp bend from the related but obviously distinctive squealing sound of skidding to a halt.

Even as I start to think about it I can feel my mind racing back over the best part of about 50 years, and in an instant I am lying on my stomach in the front room of our flat in West Norwood, eyelevel with a Ford Thunderbird belonging to Glyn Whitcomb.

Nothing was ever so coveted before or since. Also hard to believe but I mean it. Of all the things I have ever wanted, including any particular girl, guitar, holiday, job, motorbike, win on the pools or house, I think I can honestly say that I never wanted anything as badly as I wanted – as a 7-year-old – Glyn Whitcomb's scale model of a Ford Thunderbird with a built-in motor.

We're talking before Skalextric, and even before you could open the bonnet to see a shiny silver-painted representative moulding of the engine. We're talking before you could lift off the roof to examine the miniature seats and steering wheel, which in some cases might even turn. Better yet, it might even turn and be connected so as to steer the front wheels, and just how exciting is that?

No, this was a Dinky toy, plain and simple, with no moving parts other than spinning tyres and front-wheel suspension. But merely the fact that it was two-tone – pink on the bottom with a black roof – was so exotic as to take it into a different stratosphere from our everyday experience. Every car that I had ever seen in the flesh up until that point was black. Matt black.

The Ford Thunderbird was preposterously long, extraordinarily flat, unspeakably sleek, and had the most spectacular tailfins with multiple red and orange lights on the back. It had spoked wheels painted silver, and no fewer than two headlights on either side at the front. The sheer extravagance of it in an age of post-war rationing when you needed coupons to get a lamb chop and we had never seen a banana. (I don't think that either of these things is true, by the way, but at this distance it feels as though they might have been.) Anyway, the point is that this model car featured an entire chromium-surrounded headlight more than was absolutely necessary – on either side!

I feel sure that Glyn must have realised the power of my envy because I believe that he took pity on me and, on the occasion I am remembering, I think he may actually have agreed to allow me to keep the car for an overnight stay at our place. This was a big and, rather more than he probably realised, a reckless thing to do. Little did he know that I was perfectly capable of packing my meagre possessions into a spotty handkerchief, attaching it to a stick over my shoulder, and leaving the country with his Ford Thunderbird tucked into the front right-hand pocket of my short trousers. As I pondered doing so, I was determined to extract the maximum out of every available moment by viewing it with one eye shut first from this angle, and then tilting it a few degrees round so that I could admire it from that angle. Then a little bit more and a little bit more.

For hours upon hours I would push the object backwards and forwards, contorting my tongue towards the back of my mouth to produce eerily life-like throaty noises of roaring engines, cornering hard around building blocks, and thereby testing the in-built suspension to its limits. I found that if I lay quite flat, my head pressed down hard against the carpet with one eye closed, I could very easily imagine the car being full-sized, and the fact that when I stood up I felt dizzy, and sported a livid friction rash on the side of my face, was but a small price to pay for the joy of my fantasy.

Nothing was going to stop me from owning a real Ford Thunderbird when I grew up. Nothing. Maybe not in pink, because even then I knew that pink was a girly colour. Red, probably, or maybe yellow. Certainly not black. Yes, these were the 1950s, and you could have a car in any colour so long as it was black.

The Ford Thunderbird was the iconic vehicle representing a lifestyle which we could only dream of, our fantasies stimulated by rare glimpses of life as lived by Kookie in *77 Sunset Strip*. Anyone remember that? I can't remember the name of the bloke who played Kookie, but I think he worked for a nightclub which was situated next door to a private detective agency run by Stu Bailey – played by Efrem Zimbalist Jr. Honestly! Who had a name like Efrem Zimbalist Jr? No-one we knew. We were all Dennis, or Norman, or Alan, or Stephen. We were Potts or Draper or Tyler. Not a lot of Efrems round our way. Not a lot of Zimbalists. And certainly no 'juniors'.

Kookie was the personification of cool, just as cool was beginning to be a word which didn't mean the opposite of warm. For those not old enough to remember, I guess he was a sort of precursor to The Fonz, or the John Travolta character in *Saturday Night Fever*. If this is still too far back for you then probably you shouldn't be reading this book; my advice would be to put it down and go off and do something useful.

Kookie used to call girls 'chicks', which didn't do too much for me until I heard my mother saying that it was disrespectful, and so I started to do it too. Under my breath.

Mostly what Kookie used to do was to whip out a comb

at any and every opportunity to re-style his hair, sweeping it backwards in huge gestures and then patting it carefully to create the 'caves' at the front that we all wanted to cultivate. Some hope. Not with Ron the barber giving us a tuppeny all-off once a fortnight.

The relevant point about Kookie in this context is that his job was what we would now call 'valet-parking' for the nightclub. Obviously we didn't know what valet-parking was then, but it seemed like a very, very desirable job, because it meant that he spent all day leaping in and out of American cars. And being as how this was California, most of them were open-topped, which meant that leaping in and out did actually involve leaping – vaulting over the doors without opening them and landing on long bench seats made of lurid coloured plastic. How did we know that they were lurid coloured, since all this was obviously in black and white? I don't know, but take it from me, we just did.

Gear levers were conveniently attached to the steering column, presumably with the sole purpose of enabling girls to cuddle up close as you sped down the freeway. Obviously we were far too young to see any advantage in being on cuddling terms with girls, and far, far too young to see the other advantages of bench seats and column gearshifts that we would only realise many years later.

All of the cars had impossibly exotic names, like Buicks and Chevrolets and Pontiacs and Cadillacs. Oldsmobile and Dodge, Lincoln and Studebaker. They came in a whole range of pastel colours, they sported acres of chromium, and seats apparently made from the hides of beasts from the jungle. When you sounded the horn you heard the blast on two different sounds or even, heaven help us, a short tune which would irritate the bejaysus out of anyone over the age of 30. The rapture!

We looked at these American TV series and gazed upon the lifestyle they depicted with something resembling the feelings that post-Cold War Eastern Europeans must have had ten years ago when looking at us. Every day of their lives seemed to be filled with sunshine and consumer goods. Everyone seemed to be rich and (presumably because they had been chosen to be on the telly) everyone seemed to be beautiful. Boy oh boy how we wanted it, and boy oh boy was it all a long way off.

For the moment, however, as close as we could get was the Dinky toy of the Ford Thunderbird, and one or two other models, I seem to recall, but none of them quite as irresistible as the T-bird.

That's not to say that real cars, comparatively modest and pedestrian though they were, were not capable of giving us a thrill. Any kind of car was of interest in those days: truth to tell, there were not many cars about of any kind, but we had an encyclopaedic knowledge of everything that was available.

This may not be an exhaustive list, but from memory I reckon these included Rolls Royce (which we had heard about and seen in pictures, but absolutely never saw in the flesh), Bentley (which we also never saw), Rover (which we very occasionally saw), Wolseley (also very occasionally), Sunbeam (quite cool), Triumph (cooler still), Ford (a little bit more common), Morris (which felt just a little bit up-market from) ... Austin (probably the most common) and finally Vauxhall (which in those days were legendarily rust-buckets).

When we were tiny kids my Dad owned a motorbike and sidecar. The mists of time are too dense for me to recall the make with certainty, but I think that maybe if I squint back through the years I can see the word 'Ariel' written on the side of the petrol tank, at just about head height with me. I recall that it was a sort of metallic grey colour, and the sidecar was made of wood with a lid that lifted off to enable us all to climb in. Maybe my earliest memory is sitting on my mother's lap in this bloody death trap, rain lashing down in volumes which made it impossible to see a sodding thing in front of us, and peering out sideways to see a profile of my Dad looking like the pilot of a Sopwith Camel, wearing an ex-army trench coat, First World War flying helmet, and goggles.

Whether it was the realisation that we were living on borrowed time, or whether it was because his job as an insurance man began to pay a bit better, eventually the day came when my Dad came home with a proper car.

Now a lot of old bollocks is talked about kids today not appreciating what they get and people having it too easy. I can say that with some certainty because of course I've written a lot of it myself. But it's hard to get away from the fact that if you've got nothing, then anything you get is going to be a big kick. I don't have any doubt that our own kids got a great thrill out of their first roller skates or their first new bike or whatever, but I'd have to say that I feel sure they never got a thrill at the level we experienced when my Dad brought home our first family car. And so one can only imagine how excited we would have been had it actually been possible to start the engine.

I think I've recorded somewhere before that there was a hill at the side of Bligh House, which we used to career down in our home-made go-karts, risking immediate death or lifelong injury every time we reached the junction at the bottom. Another equally valuable use for this hill was that it ensured that cars could be jump-started by rolling down it – which was just as well because the batteries were always flat.

When I came home from school on the day my Dad brought home this first car, it was already parked on the hill. Large bricks were placed in front of all the wheels, because Dad had worked out that he couldn't trust the handbrake. Fresh drops of oil were already staining the tarmac underneath. It was possible to see glimpses of white canvas protruding through the rubber where the tyre tread should be.

This first car was an Austin A40 Devon, registration number BYM 44. Go onto the internet, if you can be bothered, and have a look. Then Google a Ford Thunderbird and study the difference.

However, the big difference for me was that in order to persuade myself that the T-bird was a real car I had to lie horizontal and use my all-too-vivid imagination to scale it up, while in order to achieve the dream of mobility in the Austin all I had to do was to behave myself. Not an easy task in ordinary circumstances, but a whole hell of a lot easier if the incentive was the prospect of a ride in the car.

Have you been to any of those classic car shows that turn up in rural towns through the summer? One of them is staged annually just down the road from us, and so every year we pop along with whoever might be visiting that day so that I can bore for England on the subject of 'my Dad had this' and 'this was my first ever car'. You can see anyone under the age of 30 listening to this looking at me in the same way as I used to look at the blokes who talked about riding on a horse and cart – a mixture of boredom at your dull old stories, and amazement that you can have lived so long.

The point is that when you see these cars again, 50 years

after they were the most exciting things in your life, you can't help but get a very weird feeling. Obviously they are far smaller than you remember them, but that's not surprising because you yourself were half the size you are now. The leather seat, which seemed so vast and cold underneath the backs of your legs, is now hardly wide enough to accommodate your spreading tush. Foot pedals, which were once so far away that they felt like 'one small step for man', now seem so close that your knees are grazing the steering wheel. The switches which all looked out of a sci-fi film are now entirely clumsy and clunky,

and the dials which indicated mysterious things like 'AMPS' didn't work then and don't work now.

The Austin Devon didn't last long and was replaced by an Austin A55, also in black, with registration number KYN 360. And that was replaced by an Austin A60 (996 VPJ). By the way, can you remember the registration numbers of the cars your family had when you were a kid? If you can, I'll bet you are male and over 50, and if you can't I'll bet you are not. Just a theory.

All of these cars were always going wrong in one way or another, and so when my brother and I went to Sunday School to thank God for our daily bread and for letting the British beat the Germans in the war, my Dad's weekly worship used to take place prostrate on the ground underneath these vehicles. If we were lucky, by the time we got home he would be washing the oil and grease from his hands and face, or my mother would be bandaging up the gash he had sustained while wrestling with a monkey wrench, and there would be the prospect of an outing.

During the war my mother had been evacuated from Upper Norwood, where the Crystal Palace acted as a very handy navigational aid for Hitler's bombers. They had sent her down to Hayling Island, itself handily close to Portsmouth, which was another prime military target. Quite what the point of that was has always eluded me, but the practical implication was that we had a place at the coast to visit on our Sunday outings. My mother had been taken in by a wonderful couple called Jack and Marie Hurford, who had become second parents to her, much to the chagrin actually of her real parents, but that's all another thing.

The relevant point here is that this journey used to take us to the Kingston by-pass, down the A3, and eventually around the Devil's Punch Bowl – a great big hole in the earth which my brother Steve and I always assumed had been caused when, in what must have been a terribly bad temper, the devil had punched the earth. The concept of punch as something you might drink, as opposed to receive if you didn't watch yourself, was a bit off our radar.

We always felt very relieved if we got to Hayling Island without incident. It was a long way and much could go wrong, and often did. When this happened, we were usually in for a vivid episode involving my Dad cursing and swearing and sweating beneath the bonnet or, just as often, requiring us all to get out of the car so that he could jack it up, take off a tyre and, there and then, patch an inner-tube and re-inflate the tyre with a foot-pump. Yes kids, hard though it is to believe, all this took place in the same lifetime as the one I am living now.

The tension caused by these incidents at least had the redeeming aspect that it guaranteed good behaviour on the part of my brother and I. Neither of us would dare to add further to the atmosphere, which was already at breaking point. However, sometimes, on the way back, no doubt over-tired and irritable after a long day, we would start to argue. Usually it was about him monopolising the whole of the armrest, which handily divided his territory from mine. Sometimes his foot would deliberately trespass over the transmission into my half. Sometimes one of us would find ourselves complaining, 'Mum, tell him, he's looking out of my window!' Usually the following skirmishes were allowed to go on for five minutes or so before my Dad would take his left hand off the steering wheel, half turn, and give us both a sharp and stinging slap on the bare legs. Then he would immediately command us not to cry, on pain of receiving another one. These incidents were sufficiently frequent, and also sufficiently fleeting, to have left no permanent scars.

This charming drive down memory lane won't detain us too much longer, but I do want to recall a couple of things about our annual trips to the West Country just in case they ring any bells with you.

During the school holidays, every Whit, my Dad, Mum, brother and I used to drive down to a little village called Pensilva, where we would stay for a week or two in a cottage owned by the local postman. These journeys would be the modern equivalent of driving from Southampton to Aberdeen, starting at about 4 am, taking about 9 hours, and getting us there at about tea-time.

The village was (and presumably still is) at a high altitude and more or less centrally placed between north and south coasts, so that the idea was that we would wake up in the morning, look all the way around, check in which direction the weather seemed to be most promising, and head off that way.

Whichever way we went involved driving down a very long hill as we left the village. I seem to think that petrol cost something like 1/9d or 2 shillings a gallon in those days, and therefore naturally it had to be conserved. So every morning we would play a game in which my father would get up as much speed and momentum as he could as we left the village. At the optimal moment over the brow of a hill, and with a kind of flourish that could only happen when he was in a holiday mood, he would turn off the engine. At the same time he would reset the milometer (or is it called odometer? – anyway, in those days we called it milometer) to zero.

The idea was to see how far we could go before my Dad had to restart the engine. Needless to say, these were the days before the steering would lock when you turned off the ignition, because otherwise we wouldn't have survived the first trip and you wouldn't be reading this compelling memoir. It was also the days before seat belts, air bags, or any other device designed to prevent us from ending up in the event of a crash as corned beef.

The road was narrow and had loads of bends in it, and so I feel pretty confident that we must have been risking life and limb on a daily basis as we squealed around blind corners, with my brother and I urging my father on no account to touch the brakes, and my mother gripping for dear life on to a leather strap at the side. On and on we would go, thrown hard against the doors to the left as we screamed around to the right, and thrown hard to the right as the car screeched to the left. God help anyone coming the other way, and God help us if it had ever been a combine harvester.

At one point there was a little upward incline, which would slow us right down and we would struggle to get over the brow, but if we had gained enough momentum we would be carried over it and on to the next descent. Eventually we would reach another longer incline where our progress would become slower and slower and gradually would come to a halt, and in the last few seconds my brother and I would be throwing our scrawny bodies backwards and forwards like ticking metronomes, trying somehow to add to the forward motion. Memory may be playing tricks on me, but I think the all-time record was 2.4 miles. At the end of the holiday we would add up the number of free miles, divide it by the cost of petrol, and marvel at how much money we had saved.

All terrific fun and the stuff of wonderful memories for us kids, but could you do that now? Of course not. For a whole range of no doubt very good reasons, but among them a number which make us Grumpy.

Nowadays, for example, cars are designed so that the moment you turn off the ignition, the steering will lock, with the effect that you cannot 'free-wheel' anywhere. What were once open and empty roads are these days cluttered up with road signs, and road narrows, and road works and sleeping policemen. Where once there were junctions, no doubt they have installed traffic lights or mini-roundabouts. And whereas in those days, as kids, we would have been able to add the vitally important forward thrusts of our little bodies to the momentum, nowadays kids have to be strapped into fool-proof chairs and harnesses so elaborate that they look as though they're about to be electrocuted (now there's an idea). And of course, you cannot travel 200 yards, let alone 2.4 miles, without seeing another car.

Is all that a good thing? Of course it is. Everything today is so much safer. My Dad must have been mad to do it, and for the life of me I cannot imagine what my Mother must have been thinking of to allow it. The holiday spirit must have overcome their natural caution, and of such things family tragedies are no doubt made. But lost memories of that kind are the sort of thing that makes us Grumpy. Wonderful days, in the car, with the family, which are never coming back again.

So the point of all this? Well, as those of you who have been following carefully will already know, the main cause of Grumpiness among Grumpy Old Men in particular is disappointment. Disappointment that what we hoped and were led to believe our lives would be like has not come to pass.

As little lads, in our little games of screeching around corners and mentally competing in the Indianapolis 500, we were unconsciously expressing the fundamental aspiration of all humanity. Through our play and our fantasies we lived out the basic human desire for mobility, speed, and open space. We dreamed of adventure. We dreamed of carefree days on the unending road, and (when we got just a little bit older) we dreamed of evenings in the back seat of your car in a lay-by fumbling with your girlfriend's bra strap.

What we got was gridlock. What we got was the daily chore of crawling in our air-conditioned, over-stuffed armchairs through jammed-up streets in which a realistic aspiration might be to get into 3rd gear between two sets of traffic lights. What we got was the chance to sit and simmer, breathing in the acrid stench of exhaust fumes, listening to the constant cacophony of ugly urban-sprawl which is the real soundtrack to our lives, surrounded by angry drivers, being ordered about by bad-tempered traffic cops, and just thinking 'shit, shit and shit again'.

Did someone say Grumpy? I think so.

3 You need a wave

One of the most interesting (and potentially rather dangerous) aspects of Grumpy Old Men and Grumpy Old Women is that, very often, we don't look like what we are.

What I mean by that is when ordinary non-Grumpy people look at us, they could very easily be forgiven for thinking that they are seeing a totally inconsequential old bastard going about his or her business in a semi-detached daze. A semi-senile old git dressed in grey – benign and essentially harmless, bland of appearance and bland of mind.

What they may actually be seeing is the physical containment of a seething cauldron of irritation and frustration which, with just one more tiny piece of provocation, could so easily boil over into something very ugly indeed.

I often think this when I see kids walking down the street. As anyone over the age of about 40 or 45 knows, kids don't actually see you at all. If they do happen to glance in your direction they look right through you, and, if for any reason you should actually come to their attention by accident, they react with the kind of irritation that we might reserve for a dog who wants to smell your crotch – bordering somewhere between irritation and disgust.

They're not seeing someone who, just a blink of an eye ago, was just like them. Nor is it anywhere on their radar that, in the blink of an eye, they will be just like us. When a young person looks at an older person they are seeing a different species altogether. Not a person at all, actually, but an 'old person'. Someone who might as well not exist, except sometimes in the capacity of someone who does something for them.

So that kids walking down the pavement four abreast, if you don't get out of their way, will walk right through you. Or, if they are all blocking the pavement as you try to get by, the idea that they might move to get out of your way won't occur to them. Or, if they go through a swing-door in front of you, they will let it slam closed in your face. Or, if you do happen to hold a door open for them, it's like it's been your privilege to do so. It's your lot in life to step to one side to let them through because, after all, they are young and they have inherited the world.

Funnily enough I don't think that for the most part they are being rude, even. It's just that you are invisible. Irrelevant. Not computing.

The idea that any of this might irritate or annoy you is nowhere on their personal agenda. It wouldn't occur to them that you had any feelings about it at all, and if the thought did occur to them, it would seem of no consequence. Why should they care what you think? You're old for heaven's sake – what could it possibly matter? How could it possibly matter any less?

All this is, to a certain extent, as it should be. Being young means that you believe the whole world revolves around you, as indeed so much of it does. Since every advertisement, every television programme, and a huge percentage of newspapers and magazines make young people the central target of their content, it's scarcely surprising that they should believe it. Why should you have to worry about anyone else, least of all someone twice or three times your age?

Of course there is no reason why you should have to worry. Not, at least, until the day comes. Not until the day comes when the simmering cauldron boils over. On that day ... But until that day, it's a source of amusement to think how close they actually come, without realising it. By which I mean how close they come to finding themselves splattered across the pavement.

What am I talking about? Well, the perfect opportunity to illustrate is provided by the ubiquitous pedestrian crossing.

In itself the basic idea of pedestrian crossings is not a bad one and, at least here in the UK, the rule is clear. Boiled down to its most basic it is this. If, as a motorist, your car comes in contact with any pedestrian while they are anywhere on a pedestrian crossing, it's your fault, and that's that. There are no ifs or buts. There can be no 'he ran out in front of me.' No 'the arsewipe wasn't looking where he was going.' If he's on the crossing and you run into him with your car, he is royally squished but you are royally stuffed.

This does not seem to be the case in some other countries. In France, for example, you have to wonder what is the point of a pedestrian crossing, if there is any point at all. If you, as a pedestrian in Paris, step onto one in the hope that the traffic will stop you are surely going to be violently disappointed. Indeed, disappointed may be about the best thing that can happen to you. Instead of stopping, or even slowing down, French drivers are more likely to glare at you as though you are demented, or otherwise not to take the slightest bit of notice of you at all. Maybe there is a point to the French pedestrian crossing, and if there is one and you know it please don't bother to try to enlighten me. I prefer the certainty of my prejudice.

No, in Britain, when a pedestrian puts a foot on a pedestrian crossing, no matter how unreasonable his or her behaviour might be, no matter how provocative the circumstances, he or she has the right of way. If you are in a car, or on a motorcycle, or even on a bike, you have to stop.

The woman pushing one of those very irritating jogging-strollers who is bombing down the pavement and who swerves at the last minute, ploughing across the road in front of you and causing you to screech to a halt on pain of knocking her infant into orbit? She has the right of way.

The idiot joggers who will do anything to avoid breaking their step or their pace or their heartbeat or their biorhythms or whatever it is they are monitoring so carefully with that ridiculous thing strapped to their wrist, and streak across the crossing at a jaunty 45-degree angle? They have the right of way.

The infant school teacher whose brood of 45 kids has strung out so that the stragglers are about half a mile behind the leaders, and who seems to think that her duty to molly-coddle them outweighs your duty to get to the betting shop before the 3.30 at Kempton Park? Yes, you've guessed it; she has the right of way.

And most of all. Most provocative, to the point of providing a plausible defence for justifiable homicide, are the kids with the MP3 players stuck in their ears, walking away from you down the pavement, but then striding straight onto and across the crossing without even looking up. Even they, god damn it, have the right of way.

They all have the right of way, and 999 times out of 1,000 they're going to make their crossing entirely safely. 999 times out of 1,000 they are going to be able to rely on the fact that you are essentially a harmless old sod, whose job it is to acquiesce. 999 times out of 1,000 you are going to do whatever is necessary – including braking hard and thereby throwing yourself and your passengers forward, or being hit in the back of the neck by the map-book you carelessly left on the back shelf. 999 times out of 1,000 they are going to get away with it.

They have behaved unconscionably, but you have to stop.

But this is where the danger I was talking about earlier comes in. If any of the above were to bother to glance at the driver of the car, what they would think they were seeing is a grey person in a grey suit with a grey face and a grey personality. A daft old sod. What in fact they are seeing is the human equivalent of Vesuvius, Fuji and Popocatepetl rolled into one. A scarcely contained receptacle for decades of built-up anger and frustration, whose foot is just hovering above the accelerator and who, for just two pins, would happily tap it down that critical centimetre and project them like an unguided missile into the middle of next week.

They are seeing a Grumpy Old Man, or Woman, who is so close to finally losing it that if they did but know it they are just milliseconds away from meeting their maker. Yes, that's right – the one they don't believe in.

And it could all so easily be avoided.

'You need a wave.' That was the verdict of my old friend and Grumpy Old Man of this parish Sir Gerry Robinson. 'You

just need a wave,' and if you don't get one, he posited, you should just be allowed, just now and again, to run one of them over.

It's not even the wave, actually. A glance or a nod will do. It's just the simple recognition that you exist. You may be over the age of 40 but despite that you do continue to have a right to live. Not quite as much right as they do, obviously, but at least some right.

So there we are. All these kids and inconsiderate idiots bounding or slouching or wobbling along the pavement, assuming that we're just going to stop so that they don't need even to pause in their stride, are in actual fact living far more dangerously than any of them could probably ever realise. They have no inkling whatsoever of how near I and others like me have come to just twitching the toes, just depressing the accelerator those few centimetres – just that tiniest movement of one foot, with such momentous consequences. How very, very forbidden, but nonetheless how very, very tempting.

But no. Obviously even the grumpiest of Grumpy Old Men and Women draw the line at anything so drastic. We wouldn't. We couldn't. Would we?

4 Parking

Now then, a brief diversion, if you'll forgive the expression, before we get into the detail of the various joys of trying to park your car.

I had a fairly good state-funded education, I have a degree from a pretty decent university, I have a mortgage, I brought up a family, I have run several businesses, I have understood and signed many legal contracts, I have negotiated wage deals, produced quite a lot of rather complicated TV series and written half a dozen books. *But I cannot understand the parking regulations on the high street in Wimbledon Village!*

I am serious. Anyone who knows the area will sympathise. There is a row of what appear to be parking bays just outside PizzaExpress with a machine which dispenses parking tickets. Written in tiny letters on the machine, which are scarcely legible during daylight hours and are not readable at all after dusk, is a set of rules and times and prices.

That would seem straightforward enough; however, it appears that this set of instructions and times and prices do not represent the entirety of the rules. Not at all. It seems that the stuff that is written on the ticket machine has to be read in conjunction with a little sign on a pole nearby which gives another set of times and rules. And, after as careful a study as it is reasonably possible to do while standing on the pavement and bending your knees to get close enough to read the small print, and then comparing the information gleaned with what it says on the pole, there is no way to work out which are the times you can park, and which are the times you can't park. No way to work it out at all.

Ordinarily I might feel a bit ashamed to admit that I can't understand a simple thing like a set of instructions on a parking bay, and maybe I should be. But in this case at least I am in very good company. Go there any evening, of any day, at around about 6.30 and you will see a little gaggle of people crowding around the ticket machine, scratching their heads, and asking each other if they can park or not. Most often they give up and you see them drive away, looking for somewhere else to park so they can walk back for their pizza.

However, many other more bold souls think that the complex set of instructions must mean that you *can* park in the hours listed, which could just as easily mean you *cannot* park, and take a chance. Walk past again at around 7pm, and you will usually see the cars belonging to these foolhardy folk festooned with parking tickets. I have often seen traffic wardens lurking like cockroaches in doorways, witnessing the head-scratching, only to pounce once the hapless gullible fools have rounded the corner out of sight.

No, trying to park the car is easily the most Grump-making of any aspect of Grumpy old driving. In no aspect of our daily lives is the continual battle between Grumpy Old Men and

Grumpy Old Women on the one hand, and our tormentors on the other, so constant, so relentless.

It may be that you are lucky enough to live in a town where they don't hate the motorist, and if you are so fortunate you should just spend a few minutes amusing yourself at how idiotic all the rest of us are to put up with it.

Wherever two or three of us are gathered together, there will be stories about outrageous behaviour by traffic wardens. We've all heard them. The guy who slaps a £50 fine on your windscreen because your wheel is touching the white paint outlining the border of the parking space. The woman who can see you hurrying back to the car but writes the ticket anyway three seconds after the meter goes to penalty. The meters which say '2 hours and no return for 2 hours'; where you park for 2 hours, drive around the block for 40 minutes trying to find another space, find one 100 yards from the original, park, pay, and still get a fine. Have you done all of these? You must have done. I certainly have.

If you live in London, or Manchester, Leeds, Newcastle, Cardiff, Birmingham, Edinburgh, Bristol, Glasgow, etc, etc, you'll know what I am talking about. And it's not just the biggest towns and cities; it's also Salisbury and Exeter and Sevenoaks and Hull and Leicester and Carlisle and ... well, it's just about anywhere.

If you live in one of these conurbations and drive a car, you are nothing less than the innocent enemy in a war. These places are at war against the car-driver, and they deploy armies of men and women in uniform and equipped with disabling equipment to be permanently deployed against you.

The geniuses I described in chapter 1, or their heirs or comrades, have had more fun trying to make it difficult to stop or park your car, even more than the fun they continue to have in preventing us from getting anywhere in the first place. They've had the Rio carnival, the Pamplona bull-run and Christmas at Disney all rolled into one. Oh boy, have they got their rocks off on this one. They've been at their most inventive, their creative best, and they've come up with some lulus.

First of all, there is the humble parking meter. How much frustration and heartache and bad temper and abbreviation of life span have these caused you over the years? And how many different ways have they thought of for these things to piss you off?

To start with, there is no standard agreement on what denomination of coins they will take. It seems to me that some take £1 coins and 20ps, others take 50ps and £2 coins, and occasionally you'll come across one that takes 10ps. Most often, of course, they'll gladly accept two or three of one sort of coin, and then they'll jam up and won't take anything.

You can't now move to another meter, assuming that there is one, because you've used half of your coins in this meter, and it's now stuck. So you look for a traffic warden and, astonishingly, there isn't one. Then you write a note explaining carefully what has happened and leave it on your dashboard. You were only too willing to pay, and indeed you had paid £4 already, but then you weren't allowed to pay any more.

You've been very responsible and you've done your best to pay the required price, you're parking somewhere where you are doing no harm to anyone else, and you've left a polite note to explain what has happened.

Does that work?

Of course it bloody well doesn't. When you get back to your

car, sure as eggs are eggs you are going to find a parking ticket. Why? Because you have parked at a meter which isn't working and that's that. £50. No arguments. You've broken one of their unfair, unreasonable, totally arbitrary rules and you have to pay for it. Next?

Well next is the price you have to pay at some of these bloody meters to park at all. In some areas it's 20p for an hour, and in some places it's £1 for ten minutes. Yes, that's right. £6 an hour to park your car at the side of the road. You are having to pay the equivalent of the minimum wage for a full-time employee just to be able to leave your car while you go and do something. How can that be OK? How can we have elected people who think this is alright?

Then there are the ticket machines, which have all the same issues about accepting or not accepting different coins on what seems to be a totally arbitrary basis, and these have the added complication that every second coin of any denomination goes straight through the machine and falls out of the bottom. Not always. It's not a particular individual coin it objects to, because sometimes you can put the same coin in again and it stays in, and sometimes you can't. The machine is just doing it for fun, because otherwise your life might be just a tiny bit easier.

Even when I've done everything right, I've occasionally managed to get a parking ticket by coming back to the same bay within two hours, or by leaving the ticket on the dashboard rather than sticking it to the window, or by sticking it to the window only to have it fall off onto the dashboard, or by over-staying my welcome by 90 seconds.

Notwithstanding all of the above, I have hitherto found that if I carry enough coins of enough denominations, and leave enough time to cruise around and find a free meter, I can

usually find somewhere to park in central London. However, today, even those elaborate preparations and preconditions are not enough.

No, no, not at all. The latest wheeze dreamed up by the people who are paid to make life more difficult is that you have to pay by making a phone call. Yes, that's right. The little bays have a little notice next to them displaying a phone number, and you have to phone that number, give them your credit-card details, your car registration number, your date of birth, star sign and food preferences, and then they'll let you park. OK, I'm lying about the last bits, but the general gist of it is correct.

I have to make a phone call and have a credit card in order to park my car. Anyone remember what we were saying earlier about arseholes making the simplest thing as complicated and difficult as possible?

So now you can't park around the Aldwych or anywhere around Covent Garden, or probably loads of other places, unless your mobile phone is handy, topped up, and you've remembered your credit card. Is it only me that thinks this is total bloody insanity? Is the world sane and I've gone mad, or the other way around? I just don't know any more.

What if I don't have a sodding credit card? What if I don't want to carry a mobile phone? Jesus H. Christ! Will someone, somewhere, give us a break? No? I guess I should have realised.

But let's calm down a bit. Parking on the street is not always the only option. Surely there are other alternatives that are less vexatious than parking meters, ticket machines and phone calls?

Take, for example, the multi-storey car park. If you're over the age of 50 or so, believe it or not multi-storey car parks feel like a relatively recent development. I think I remember the first one in the area to spring up on Bromley High Street when I was a kid. Along with the advent of Wimpy Bars and shopping arcades (we hadn't yet started to call them 'malls') the multi-storey car park felt like it was part of the gradual Americanisation of our society. Multi-storey car parks were frequently the scenes of dramatic scenes in movies. A good hide-out for a sniper – as in those Clint Eastwood movies. Or for throwing someone off the top of, as in *Get Carter*. Or for a bloody good car chase, as in *The Bourne* this or that, or just about every Bond movie. Or for providing an opportunity for any character with suicidal tendencies to leap from, as in too many films to count.

So why, can anyone help me to understand, do the

stairwells of multi-storey car parks always smell of piss? Does anyone know the answer to this? It's not just sometimes – they *always* smell of piss.

Seriously. It's the case in Soho and Salisbury, in Manchester and Milton Keynes. Every multi-storey car park you ever go into smells of piss. Even those run by someone who gives a damn. Why is that, do you think?

I think I know the answer, but let's eliminate a few things first, should we?

Could it be that by the time you've parked and are on your way to the shops it's taken so long that you just cannot wait any longer? Maybe, but I sort of doubt it.

Is it some sort of strange human reaction to driving up and down all those ramps? Or to cruising around in so many circles? Or to all that concrete? Does any of this sort of thing act as a diuretic and bring on an uncontrollable urge to wee? Not that anyone could guess.

No, my personal theory is that it's what happens when you piss people about.

People in general, and Grumpies in particular, hate being pissed about. Being pissed about is a big part of modern life, and multi-storey car parks are not right up there with the big vexations, but they do represent quite a few of them.

For example, you always have to queue to get in them, and we hate queuing. All of the concrete barriers and obelisks mean that you are wary of stopping too close to the ticket machine, and you can't quite reach the red button out of the window. So you have to open the car door just a little bit and lean out, making you feel awkward and uncomfortable. You press a button for the ticket and it never comes right away, but always comes just as you have pushed the button requesting assistance, and the tired and tinny voice comes on the intercom just as you have solved the problem.

Then you drive, round and round and round, and every time you see a space two rows away and head for it, by the time you reach it some other arse has reversed into it. And having gone down that row towards the space which is now filled means you are joining the back of a queue of cars which came into the car park behind you.

It's about now that you start cursing the bastards who have sold you a ticket to come into the car park, irrespective of the fact that there seem to be no spaces to be had. You have no choice but to go up and up and up, only eventually to discover that you are now on the roof and there are loads of spaces.

But like all spaces in all multi-storey car parks they aren't really big enough, and they aren't really accessible enough for a car. So you have to squeeze in too close to the car on your left, with the result that your passenger won't be able to get out. Or too close to the car on the right, so that you won't be able to get out yourself. And if you or your passenger are able to get out, you can't avoid brushing down the side of your car or the neighbouring car, transferring all the mud and dirt from it to you.

Once parked and out of the car, you can never find the optimal route to the stairwell and just when you eventually reach the stairwell you'll see a sign that asks 'have you got your ticket with you?' because you can't pay on exit and need to visit the 'pay-station' before returning to your car. So you go back and squeeze down the side of the car again, contorting yourself like a sodding limbo dancer to reach into the centre console to retrieve the ticket.

Now you are ready to exit the car park and you are feeling

stressed, put upon, and generally just pissed about by the system. And so what I think must happen is that a surprisingly high proportion of visitors to multi-storey car parks, whether consciously or unconsciously, react to being pissed about by wanting to respond in kind. So they take a piss in the stairwell.

Is this plausible? I don't know, but if it isn't, someone else will have to come up with a more credible explanation for why it is the case that every multi-storey car park in the land smells of wee. What we can all agree on is that they do.

All that said, multi-storeys are just one of the alternative ways in which the whole business of parking provides a consistent torment for all of us, but for Grumpies in particular. That's not to say that Grumpies are especially picked out for persecution; it's just that we are pre-disposed to be irritated, even if there isn't much to be irritated about. So when there genuinely is something, it's all so much worse.

5 Nuremberg

OK, so let's put it on the record, shall we? Let's be very clear so that no-one has any doubt, and can't say in the future that they were not warned.

The Nuremberg defence didn't work for the guys who flicked the switches in the gas chambers and, come the day, it isn't going to work for the guys who put a clamp on your car when you've just popped into the post office to buy a stamp. Nor is it going to work for the guys who wait for you to walk round the corner and tow away your car.

'Only following orders,' didn't keep the SS guys off the gallows, and it's not going to keep these guys out of the firing line either.

It's another of those aspects of our modern lives where we've come to be so intimidated, so beaten down, so resigned, so pathetic, that we accept it as 'one of those things'. Sure, we lose our temper, sure we may rant, and rave, and complain about it for days and weeks on end. But at some level we basically accept that it's OK for someone to come along and steal your car. 'One of those things'.

Well it isn't. The system of British justice works by consent, and on the basic premise that – by and large – the punishment is in line with the crime. We accept a certain tariff of punishment for a burglary, and another one for an assault, and another one for a murder and so on – and on the odd occasion that some judge doesn't really think that rape is a proper crime it makes the front page lead in the tabloids.

We're British. We have a sense of fair play. We like there to be some approximation between what you did wrong and the price you have to pay. I think we call it justice.

So how do we get to a situation in which you can stop for five minutes on a single yellow line, just to pop into the post office to renew your TV licence, not hurting or even inconveniencing anyone else, and when you come out someone has stolen your car? How did that become possible? When did that become OK?

I don't know if you have ever had your car towed away – how could I? But if you have, you'll know that it's not merely the shock that your car is missing. It's not the worry as you try to ascertain whether or not it's been stolen. It's not the extraordinary inconvenience that you've left your briefcase in the boot and it contains a lot of papers you need for the vitally important meeting that you were on your way to. It's not the problem you have in locating the police pound to which they've towed your car. It's not the finding a bus or a taxi or a tube to get you there. It's not that it's always in bandit country – a part of town you would usually go to enormous trouble to avoid. It's not the waiting around for hours on end while a lot of other hapless sods also wait around in total despair that their entire month's disposable income is going down the drain. No, it's not any of that.

It's that at every stage in the process you are being dealt with by the system like you are a paedophile. Like you've committed some heinous and unforgivable crime, which justifies these bastards in treating you with total contempt, with no suggestion of any elementary courtesy, decency, or consideration. You are treated like a bloody criminal just for leaving your car at the side of the road for five minutes. That's what really pisses you off.

Basically what this comes down to is extortion. They're going to kidnap your means of transport, and not going to let you have it back until you hand over an extraordinary sum of money. And, even if you are able and willing to do so right now,

they're going to make you hang about for as long as they like before you can get away.

And where does it say that's OK? In the bye-laws. Oh really? Yes, if you look at clause 5, paragraph 3 sub-section (ii) little b), it says that if you transgress one of their petty, totally capricious, completely arbitrary made-up rules, then they can take whatever action they like against you and you can do nothing about it. In fact, the more you rant and rave, and plead and beg, and the more of any of that you do the more it's going to make their day.

Because that's what they live for. Just to ruin your day.

So when you see those TV programmes featuring a pair of bailiffs who clamp your car and hold it to ransom until you pay an old parking fine, and you see one of them positively enjoying all-but-tricking people into looking away while the other one sneaks up and puts a clamp on their cars, turn over to the other channel. It's not funny, and it's not clever. These people are the storm troopers of modern Britain. They're bastards and they don't deserve ... well, obviously I can't write what I'm thinking. That would be turning from Grumpy to Angry, and that would never do.

No – treat these bloody people with total contempt, and most of all do your very best not to make their day by giving them even the most flimsy of excuses to clamp you or tow you away.

At least until the revolution.

6 Big Brother

The Republican Guard of Grumpiness, as I have frequently pointed out, is aged between 35 and 54 years old. The theory is that if you are younger than 35, you probably haven't had enough disappointment, seen enough absurdity, been sufficiently ground down by bullshit, really to appreciate the underlying causes of Grumpiness. Nor indeed what Grumpiness can do for you. And if you are older than 54, the thesis goes, then you should just be beginning to mellow a bit.

Neither of these parameters is hard and fast. Since we first identified Grumpiness as a clinical syndrome, I have had drawn to my attention many cases of Grumpy traits and tendencies occurring in people as young as 25. Quite often these are the sons and daughters of Grumpies, giving rise to the conjecture that the syndrome may be genetic.

Equally often, however, they have arisen spontaneously where there has been little or no sign of Grumpiness in the family hitherto. Indeed, I was rather a precocious Grumpy myself, and looking back on it with the gift of hindsight I don't think either of my parents necessarily exhibited the classic signs. Yet I can now see that I started developing some of the indicators – failing to suffer fools gladly, a tendency to point out naked Emperors, etc – not long after leaving university.

Having now emerged out of the far end of the core years, I and my family have of course been hoping for any hint that I am leaving the flaming intensity of my Grumpiness behind me, and looking forward to the onset of increasing calm. Occasional appeals to those around me have, alas, brought forth no indication that anyone sees me becoming less of an irascible and cantankerous old bastard. If there is ever any sign of progress, I will of course report it.

Within the 20-year span of radical Grumpiness, though, there is of course a vast range – and one aspect of the differences between extremes of age is those who first read George Orwell's 1984 when it was a date in the distant future, and those who read it when it was a date around then or even in the past.

When I first read 1984, in about 1966, it all seemed like a very long way off, and it felt like a very terrifying prospect. A world in which we were all surveilled by the authorities the whole of the time. A world in which anyone you met could be a secret policeman or an informer of some kind. A world in which politicians would tell us all to believe one thing one day, and tell us to believe the opposite the next day, and we were all supposed to forget that it had previously been the other way around. A world in which Big Brother was a constant and evil presence in our lives.

Can you see this coming?

For me and my generation, surprisingly naive as we must have been, I think that a lot of us almost breathed a sigh of relief when the year 1984 eventually came around. By and large we didn't feel spied on from dawn to dusk. Mrs Thatcher was the prime minister and, although she was a dreadful old baggage who made many of us ashamed to travel abroad where we might meet foreign people who would ask us whether we voted for her, she seemed a long way from Big Brother. Though there was much that was wrong with the world, we were not at war with most of it and indeed, while of course at the time we didn't know it, we were only five years from the fall of the Berlin Wall.

However, that was then, and as 1984 turned into 1994 and 2004 and beyond, it turns out that Orwell didn't get the predictions wrong. What he got wrong was the date. All the stuff that he predicted would happen 25 years ago is actually happening now and, as in his book, most of us are too stupid or distracted or complacent to recognise it. With the exception, of course, of we Grumpies.

It goes way outside the parameters of this book and my competence to analyse the military and foreign policy parallels. Suffice it to say that I remember when the Shah of Iran was a good thing, and then a bad thing, and now (maybe) a good thing again. I remember when the Russians were our enemies, then our friends, and now (for some reason only the politicians can guess at) we're building a whole new range of missiles all across what was once the Iron Curtain, which we're pointing at them. I remember being friendly with the Argentinians, then at war with them, and then friendly again. Chinese, Vietnamese, the list goes on.

Back at home, I think it is impossible quite to comprehend the level at which we are all watched and monitored, step by step, move by move, 24 hours a day. Not just by the tens of thousands of video cameras which are everywhere around us from the moment we leave our homes to the moment we turn off the lights, and sometimes maybe even beyond. Also electronically – through how we spend our money, through the people we speak to on our mobiles, through GPS, and through who and what we access on the internet.

Of course for ordinary people – those fortunate enough not to be plagued by Grumpiness, none of this is a problem. 'If you've got nothing to hide,' I hear them say, 'there should be no problem.' And anyway, they add, it's for our own good.

Well – say Grumpies in response – what if I *have* got something to hide? What if I have got something to hide that is nothing to do with anyone else, but I just don't want someone watching me doing it? Or what if I haven't got anything to hide but just don't appreciate the idea of some red-neck arsehole sitting in a booth somewhere watching me do nothing in particular? What then? I don't especially have anything to hide when I am taking a bath or having a shit, but I don't particularly want anyone looking at me. And I don't especially have anything to hide when I am walking down the street or buying a new shirt, and I don't particularly want anyone looking at me then either.

But I have no say in the matter. If I want to drive through London or any town or city of any significant size anywhere in Britain, I will have my picture taken dozens and dozens of times. If I walk through a shopping mall, my picture will be taken and automatically compared against a database of faces of people who for some reason they don't like. If I drive up the motorway, my progress can and will be monitored by scores of people in uniforms. Sometimes they will be police uniforms, sometimes security people, sometimes they will just be people in shops, offices, hotels or garages.

I'll give you an example – and I know that I'm taking a little while to get to our main theme – but I think it's worth the brief detour.

When I was doing interviews for the last series of *Grumpy Old Men*, one of the things that Nigel Havers complained about was that petrol stations have now become supermarkets. What this means is that when you are in a hurry and just want to throw down your £20 for the fuel you have dispensed from pump number 8, the person in front of you is doing their weekly shopping. And while you are in the queue behind them (according to Rick Wakeman) they always want to send their daughter back into the aisles to get a box of tampons.

Anyway, we had done the interview with Nigel and so I wanted to shoot some pictures of just such a garage to illustrate his point. We only needed a few quick shots so I positioned myself on the pavement on the south side of Hammersmith Bridge, just opposite the petrol station. I shot the thing from one angle, and then shot the thing from another angle, and after a few minutes I became aware of someone coming from the garage and walking towards me. I continued about my business and eventually this bloke arrived alongside.

If these aren't the actual words of the conversation, then I swear they are as close as makes no difference. This is what life is like in Britain in 2008.

'Do you mind telling me what you are doing?'

Actually I did mind telling him what I was doing, but at this point I was still trying to be nice.

'I am just taking some pictures of your garage.'

'What for?'

I might have been willing to tell him at this point, but he was coming over all stroppy and aggressive, and so I didn't.

'I don't think I have to tell you that.'

There was a pause. This was not what he was expecting. He was hoping that I did have to tell him that, but for the moment he couldn't think why. Eventually he altered tack just a bit.

'Have you got permission?'

'I don't need permission.'

'Yes you do.'

'No I do not.'

'Yes you do.'

'From whom?'

'From me or from the owners of the garage.'

'Well I certainly don't have permission from you, because I guess if you had given me permission you would probably know it. And I certainly don't have permission from the owners of the garage because I haven't asked for it.'

'Why not?'

'Because I am standing on the public pavement, taking pictures of a building which is available to the public, and which any member of the public who might see my pictures could come here and see for themselves.'

'Well you should have asked for permission.'

'Why?'

'Because you cannot just take people's pictures without asking them.'

OK, so we have taken a long time to get here, but at last we have arrived ...

'Now just a minute,' I said. 'As it happens, I buy my petrol from your garage. You guys take a picture of every single car and person who comes into your garage to buy fuel. I know this because, as a motorcyclist, I have even been required to remove my crash helmet before you will switch on the tanks so that you can take my picture before I can buy my petrol. And you have got the nerve to tell me I can't film your building from the pavement?'

And this is why a lot of non-Grumpy people hate Grumpies.

However, the point of raising the subject of 1984 wasn't about being surveilled by petrol stations or the government, it's about being lied to by the government. It's about seeing something with our own eyes, but being told the opposite by the government – and being required to believe it. Worse still, it's about seeing something with our own eyes, being told it is not so, and *actually* finding ourselves believing that it is not so.

All of which irritating meandering brings us around to the Congestion Charge.

The Congestion Charge is one of the biggest scams – maybe THE biggest scam – pulled on the public by the authorities in my lifetime. When I first heard about it, I assumed it was a joke. We already pay income tax, local rates, road tax, tax for the MOT, tax on petrol and VAT on everything from engine oil to new tyres, just to be allowed to drive our cars on shitty, pot-holed and congested roads. None of us wants to drive into London anyway, and when you do have to do so there is nowhere to park. If and when you do find somewhere to park, it's like a mugging.

So here was someone suggesting that on top of the tax and the rates and the road tax and the petrol tax and the car parking, we should pay £5 a day (initially) and now a momentous £8 for the privilege of enduring this bloody nightmare that we didn't want to do anyway. Who in their right minds would want to drive in London if they had a viable choice?

That's £8 a day – £40 for a five-day working week, £2,000

a year after tax – just to be able to drive to work (on which we will pay income tax) in London!

Having realised eventually that the proposal was not intended as a joke, I still thought I could afford to find it amusing because I knew that no-one would vote for it. Who would volunteer to pay a tax to be able to do something they don't want to do anyway? But that, if I may be allowed to say so, was uncharacteristically naive of me.

What I hadn't instantly understood is that the people who would be voting would not be the people who would be paying. The people who would be voting would largely be the people who live inside the zone and therefore do not pay the tax. These people were being asked to vote for whether *someone else* should pay a tax from which they would be exempt, and indeed would benefit. That's a much easier one. Would I like someone else to pay a tax that I don't have to pay? Not difficult at all; where do I put my cross?

So installing the kit and collecting the tax is a high-tech nightmare, which introduces a whole new way in which the rest of us are spied on, monitored and oppressed by the authorities. Collecting the Congestion Charge is the most expensive method of collecting taxes anywhere in the world but shows no mercy. Cross the line one minute before 6.00pm without having paid the charge, and you're going to pay a fine. It's ruthless, it's relentless, it's anything else unpleasant beginning with r.

But would it work? Would charging people to drive their cars into London thin out the traffic and make life easier for those who could afford it, or had to afford it, one way or another? Well common sense would tell you that it would. Charging people to do something is not rocket science. You could charge

£500 a day and solve the traffic problem overnight. Presumably charging £5 or £8 wouldn't be quite that drastic, but would be likely to have an effect. It seemed likely that lots of people who currently drove into London would not be able to afford to pay yet another £8 a day to go to work, so they would either find another way to get to work, or stop going to work altogether. Result.

OK, so this is where the scam-of-the-century comes in, because if you ask the authorities whether the Congestion Charge has worked in the stated intention of reducing congestion they will tell you that it has. I heard on the radio only yesterday that traffic congestion has increased in every part of Britain except Inner London. It's taken as a given. However, at the same time, every single person who drives in London on a regular basis will tell you that it hasn't worked in affecting traffic. Or rather, they will tell you that it has had an effect – and the effect it has had has been to make the traffic worse.

Yes that's right. London has become the showpiece of the world. Bureaucratic bastards and their political masters have come from every major city on the globe to see and admire the pioneering traffic-control system which manages to raise such huge sums in taxes for the local authorities and – as each of them is no doubt told – also manages to ensure that fewer cars come into London than came in before.

Which may be true. It may be that fewer cars do come into the Congestion Zone than previously: I don't know that for sure. However, what I do know for sure is that, once inside, the cars that pay the charge move around more than they did previously.

Once upon a time if you had struggled to get into town, and maybe fought to get a parking space, once there you were probably going to remain ensconced until it was time to drive home. If you had a journey to do around London, chances were that you would walk, or get the bus, or the tube, or a taxi. Leave the car safely parked where it was for the whole day.

However now – well, you've paid to come into the Congestion Zone, so you sure as hell are going to get your money's worth. You've also been told that fewer cars are coming into the zone, so that local journey may be just as easy by car as by bus, tube or on foot. So that, once inside the zone, more people are using their cars to get around, with the result that congestion inside the zone is every bit as bad, and indeed mostly worse than it ever was before.

Meanwhile, so many people are going to inordinate lengths to avoid actually entering the Congestion Zone that all the surrounding areas and approach roads are clogged up massively – more than ever they were clogged up before the charge.

Therefore the combination of more vehicle movements inside the zone, and far more traffic on the perimeter of the zone, means that driving in and around London is now tangibly worse than it was before we were charged £8 a day for the privilege of doing so.

And here's the rub. We're told on a regular basis by Big Brother that the Congestion Charge has worked in reducing traffic congestion in London. And at the same time it is simply not possible to sit on the Euston Road at 4pm going in either direction and believe for a second that this is so. I just don't believe that there is any single person whose commute into London by car is easier now than it was before the Congestion Charge. It just isn't, but we're told that it is. Which defines the phrase 'adding insult to injury'. If it's not bad enough that we're being fined for going to work, we're being told to be

grateful for it. Told that we are better off when we can see that we are not.

Oh yes, *1984* was a bit late in coming, but it is here. Orwell's nightmare of being watched, checked up on, told what to think and consistently lied to, has arrived. And most of us are too complacent or too stupid to know, or if we do know, to care.

Unless of course you are a Grumpy. Grumpy Old Men and Grumpy Old Women. We know. Probably not much we can do about it, but blimey, we certainly aren't going to shut up about it. Unless of course someone puts a rat in a cage.

7 The first time

One of the reasons that thinking about cars and driving makes Grumpy Old Men and Women grumpy, is that they were the source of all those 'firsts' which were so wonderful at the time but which, by definition, are never coming again.

Know what I mean? All those motoring-related firsts, which gave us so much joy earlier in life, are behind us, and the truth is that it's very unlikely that you could think of a new 'first' which would give you anything near as much of a thrill. Nothing will ever quite equal some of those life-changing moments which are for ever imprinted on the A–Z of your autobiography.

What sort of thing? Well, many and variously they were:

Your Dad's first car (if you were alive then).

Your first time behind the wheel (and actually moving).

Your first solo drive – (swiftly followed by first sexual experience in a car).

Your first car of your own.

Your first new car.

… and that's probably about it.

I have a clear and vivid memory of each of them, and I am guessing that most people have probably got at least 3 out of 5. Maybe you'd be able to add to them – perhaps you are someone who could add 'first time driving Formula 1' or 'first time driving a Chieftain tank', but I wouldn't mind betting that you'd be hard pressed to add significantly to the list. Not if you were genuinely confining it to the really serious thrills.

So which of these is the greatest driving moment of all? It's a stiff competition actually, but taking everything into account I'm guessing that the greatest experience which cars and driving deliver to our short unhappy lives is the first car of our own. Be it an old banger or an Oldsmobile, a jalopy or a Jaguar. Yep. Your own car. Your own freedom. Your wheels. Your very own keys to the highway.

It's sitting there, parked outside, awaiting your command, and ready to whisk you away to anywhere you want to go, day or night, week in week out. If you want to go out for a beer, you can. If you want to go down to Bournemouth, you can. If you want to just up and sod off on a trip around the world … well obviously you can't, but you feel as though you might be able to. At the very least you can wait until someone you want to impress is within earshot and call out 'has anyone seen my car keys?'

No more 'can I borrow the car Dad?' followed by 'no, because you didn't wash it when I asked you to.' Or 'no, because you didn't do your homework.' Or seasonal blues caused by the fact that you can't use the car 'cos you didn't work late.

When you get your first car, you've arrived. Or left. Or something. Anyway, the point is, it's a milestone. The biggest of your driving life and one of the biggest of your life overall.

So what was yours? A Mini Cooper S? MGB? Triumph Dolomite? Ford Thunderbird?

Mine was a Heinkel. What the hell was that? A Heinkel. Don't pretend you don't remember. It was a bubble car. The Heinkel was a bit like the Trojan, and both were different again from the Messerschmitt. It was a three-wheeler – two at the front and one at the back, with a single door at the front, which swung out and up. This Heinkel had a bench seat for the driver and passenger, which was useful in all sorts of ways, and another little seat in the rear above the engine, which was less useful unless you had a friend who was radically vertically-challenged or shaped like Quasimodo.

The great thing about these vehicles, apart from the fact that they kept you dry, was that you only needed a motorcycle licence to be able to drive them. Essentially they were thought of as a closed-in motorbike, except that to drive them was exactly like driving a car.

Like every other kid my age, I had passed my test on a Vespa about two minutes after I was sixteen. Also, like every other kid my age, I damned nearly killed myself a dozen times riding the thing like a bloody menace. The combination of tiny wheels, roads that seemed to be constantly wet or icy, and a kid in a hurry is a dangerous brew.

I wasn't a 'mod' but I did use to wear a parka to keep out the worst of the cold. And it's difficult to believe it now but in those prehistoric days very few of us used to wear a crash helmet. Not, I don't think, because we felt it was a bit cissy to wear one. Not even, I don't think, because we thought it made us look like burks. In my case I just didn't own one, and probably thought my weekly spends were better used buying the latest album from Cream or John Mayall's Bluesbreakers.

The result was that I was constantly walking around with hair that looked as though I'd had a sudden and very serious electric shock, and ears which most of the time were so luminous from the cold that they could double as a warning for low-flying aircraft. Have you got a mental picture of this? Looking back on it, I think I can see why I was such a tremendous hit with the girls.

I recall a couple of mishaps – I came off the scooter on a wet road going round a corner and was lucky to miss the approaching milk float by a pubescent whisker. On another occasion I failed to stop in time and bumped into the back of the number 54 bus from Elmers End to Beckenham. However, at that age you feel invulnerable, and so it wasn't the imminent risk of catastrophic accident which propelled me towards getting a roof over my head. Not so much. It was more that a car, any car, seemed to provide so much more potential for pulling girls. And, once pulled, so much more flexibility about what might be done with them.

I spotted this bubble car from a small ad in *Exchange & Mart* and somehow got myself over to a dodgy-looking address in north London. The asking price was £50, but all I could scrape together was £40, and I hoped that the idea of cash and a quick deal would prove irresistible. It did, but on mature reflection I reckon that this was probably more because the guy couldn't wait to get rid of the car and I looked too much of a sucker to be allowed to walk away.

This Heinkel was painted dark blue, looked fairly smart,

and was a death trap. Leaving aside the fact that there was an overpowering smell of petrol inside from a leaking fuel tank, it was of course desperately unstable and prone to being bounced about by the slightest gust, like a table-tennis ball in a hurricane.

One of my first priorities was to show it off to my girl-friend, so, before even properly familiarising myself with the thing, I immediately set off to drive it down to visit her where she was at university in Canterbury. The wind was high and I spent most of the time wrestling with the steering wheel in my attempt to stay out from under the wheels of trans-continental juggernauts that would have squashed me like an infant hedgehog under a steam roller and not even noticed the bump.

Anyway the main point of mentioning the Heinkel is that this was how I learned to drive. Driving the bubble car required spatial awareness and gear changing and clutch control, and all the things that usually defeat learners, so that by the time I booked my test for my 18th birthday I was driving like a veteran. These were the days before things like the separate written section, and before sensible ideas like making you drive on a bit of dual carriageway.

So now I was ready to be off. The only trouble was that I didn't have wheels. Well, I had three of them, but by now three wheels very definitely felt like one too few.

I was still a relatively penniless student but my brother Steve had a job and was making some proper money, so the agony I felt about not owning a car was made considerably worse by the fact that he owned and drove a whole series of cars which were exactly those that any sensible red-blooded young male most coveted. Not the T-bird of course, but certainly several of the British equivalents.

When I first passed my driving test he owned a grey and white Mini Cooper S and, to be fair to him, he did occasionally loan it to me. This was particularly generous because, of course, we all drove like bloody lunatics. I mean like madmen, and these were the days before seat belts, and also before anyone had properly worked out that it wasn't a great idea to do a lot of drinking and driving.

Though we didn't get on too well as kids, the truth is that my brother has always been a good egg, so I don't feel too proud to be confessing something I did way back then. (And when he reads this, it's going to be the first he has known of it.)

He was due to go on holiday for a week or so, somewhere out of the country, and the question arose as to whether I could use the Mini while he was away. I recall having the hots for a particular girl at the time, and feeling certain that use of the car in this crucial period was my ticket to paradise. For days on end I could think of little else except the car and the girl. The girl and the car. The car and the girl. OK, OK, I was obsessed.

First of all he said I couldn't use the car at all. I was crushed, but didn't feel able to tell him the particular reason because I don't think that assisting my sex life was especially high on his agenda of priorities. Especially not if it in any way involved the rear seats of his car. Then for some reason he relented, but said he wanted to limit my use of it. He decreed that during his absence I couldn't travel more than 200 miles. He would make a note of the mileage before he went and, if I exceeded his limit, I wouldn't be allowed to use the car again.

I begged and I pleaded. 200 miles in a week? I could get through that in a day. That was the point, of course. He didn't want me tearing up the countryside in his precious motor, and who can blame him?

Anyway that was the final agreement and, needless to say, I got to about 180 miles within the first two days. However, this was before I was due to take this girl out at the weekend. I struggled with my conscience for an hour or two – well, maybe only just a minute or two – but eventually managed to overcome my scruples. I whipped up the bonnet, detached the cable leading to the back of the speedo, and continued to drive without clocking up any extra recorded miles for the rest of the holiday.

Naturally I reattached the speedo cable on the morning my brother was due to return, notched up just a few miles so we got to a very plausible 187 or something, and presented him with his keys when he got home.

'187 miles,' I said. 'Not a mile over.'

'Ha ha,' he said, in triumph. 'I didn't check the mileage before I left.'

'You bastard,' I said. 'I've been bloody paranoid about that. Measuring every mile. It's been sitting at the kerb for the last three days.'

I never told him. 'Til now. I guess we sort of deserved each other. And yes, while natural discretion and concern for the reader's sensitivities prevent me from revealing any details, suffice to say that the use of the car fulfilled its intended purpose.

Anyway, the Mini Cooper went like the proverbial bat out of hell. Anyone remember those tiny, tiny steering wheels? God knows what we were thinking of. Some of them were about ten inches across and wouldn't have been suitable to steer a bumper car, let alone an over-powered speed machine with acceleration like a space rocket and brakes like a very fast vehicle with very poor brakes.

And while we're on the subject, does anyone remember how cool it was to buy those little extensions to the switches on the instrument panel? Four inches of black plastic, which fitted over the little flickers? Just how sad and pathetic is it to think back to the kick we got out of extending these switches so that, presumably, we wouldn't have to lean forward to turn on the windscreen wipers? A lot has changed in 40 years, I think, but the fact that in those days it would make your day to buy and attach four bits of black plastic to lengthen a switch on your car dashboard sort of says it all.

Eventually my brother traded in the Mini Cooper for a still more enviable MGB GT in British racing green. Now that was a very fine car. Being of the slightly taller persuasion, it was the first car in which I experienced having to more or less sit down on the pavement to manipulate my legs into the space, and then shift my bum onto the low-slung seats. If you made the mistake of getting one leg in, and then putting your backside on the seat, it proved impossible to bend the other leg enough to be able to tuck it in. Several seconds of awkward manipulation and contortions would precede defeat, and you would have to get out of the car and start again. Not great when your main objective was to impress.

Anyway, if anything this MGB went even faster than the Mini and, thank God, was a little bit more stable round the corners. A bit closer to the ground. Leaving aside the exigencies of getting in and out, it was of course fantastic for pulling women, and utterly useless for doing anything at all with them once you had.

This one had leather bucket seats, walnut dashboard, a built-in radio, and a very short gear stick. All trivial details, no doubt, to anyone who doesn't remember the tactile thrill of settling down into your driving position, jabbing the gear lever into first, and the almost tangible sound from the inappropriately named silencer, which made a noise like the second coming of Christ, except obviously far more dramatic.

After that my brother went to live in Spain for a summer while I went to university, and was obviously far too poor to afford a car of my own. However, my mother was of a generation of women who came late to driving, if they came to it at all, so she was at best a tentative and unconfident motorist. This, and her selfless love for me, meant that I was able to take advantage of her goodwill even to the extent of occasionally borrowing her car and taking it 300 miles away for much of the academic term. Leaving her with all the bills and none of the wheels – the kind of deal only a mother would accept.

The first vehicle to come under this arrangement was a Morris 1000. Black, and looking exactly like the mental picture you probably have in your mind right now. The Model T Ford of British cars. Sturdy, steadfast, mostly utterly reliable, and as dull as the red galvanising paint which kept the galloping rust at bay at the bottom of the doorsills. But hey, who was complaining? It went along, it kept me dry, and it was at my disposal. OK, it wasn't the T-bird, but I wasn't Kookie either. I was a long-haired layabout student with only a local authority grant and the money I could earn during the holidays to live on. And of course the odd fiver received in the post from my mother, and never properly appreciated or acknowledged. Sorry Ma.

In comparison to the cars belonging to some other students, this black Morris 1000 was relatively a limo. A mate of mine had the convertible version of the same car, which was great except for the fact that, as students of physics or engineering will tell you, the main challenge facing designers of convertibles is the integrity of the shape.

A normal car is like an egg, with the overall structure supported in the round. With no roof, a convertible needs to be very strong indeed in the chassis to compensate. This was no doubt a challenge in those relatively early days of car design even when all was going well. If you add the fact that every aspect of a vehicle is in an advanced state of corrosion, it can lead to an interesting situation.

What it meant as a practical matter for this Morris 1000 convertible was that the car doors were an essential part of what remained of the integrity of the structure, and it was imperative to keep them closed at all times if the shell of the car was to remain rigid. Are you with me? If anyone forgot and made the mistake of opening the doors, the whole car would literally sag in the middle, and then it would not be possible to get them closed again. We tried to ensure that this happened as seldom as was practical, which meant that we had to find alternative ways of getting in and out of the car.

I seem to think that one or two of us might have been able to climb in and out through the windows. I, myself, was three stone lighter then than I am now, but even then I don't think this was possible for me. I, and others of a more than average scale, used to have to climb in and out via the convertible canvas roof.

From time to time one of us would forget, or be too ine-briated, or find it necessary to vomit without clear notice, and would inadvertently open a door. As soon as that happened the car would drop down a couple of inches in the middle, so that we'd all have to get out and position two blokes on one side, and two blokes on the other. Then each of us would place our hands under the car and, using a mix of amazing manual dex-terity and coordination, we would lift the whole thing on its springs. Only after we had raised it an inch or so would we be able to close the doors and thereby restore some solidity to the structure.

None of this was easy to coordinate at the best of times when we were sober. However, this was something which seldom happened when we were sober, and was especially not easy to do when all four of us were as drunk as skunks and also laughing hysterically at the fact that we were in this position once again.

Oh happy days.

The first proper car I actually owned was, of course, a VW

Beetle. In a very appealing shade of beige. It was in my last year at university and I had made quite a bit of money working on building sites. I seem to think this car cost about £350.

Looking back on it and knowing what I know now, I feel fairly certain that at some point in its recent history, this car must have been involved in a very serious accident. When I bought it, it had recently been re-sprayed, which in itself should have made me suspicious. Instead, of course, all it did was make the car seem more attractive because it looked smart and almost new instead of the write-off it most probably was.

Inevitably things started to go wrong fairly quickly – mostly with the structure. In particular the bottom of the doors rusted out altogether, so that the inside framework of the door was not actually attached to the outside panel, thereby causing an alarming rattle at low speeds, and an even more alarming flapping around at anything over about 40 mph.

I feel I can say with complete confidence that my way of dealing with this will bring back the same recollections to a whole generation of Grumpies of around my age and level of prosperity. All those bloody hours spent fiddling about with those sodding fibre-glass compounds of one kind or another, trying to patch up the rusting bodywork of cars which were mostly decaying faster than we could fill in the holes.

Do you remember? You'd have to squeeze out a line of this stuff from the big tube, and alongside it a line of equal length of stuff from the little tube. Then you would mix them together with a little plastic spatula. I could never find quite the right thing to mix them on, and in the process there was the ever-present fear of being asphyxiated by the overwhelming, and what seemed to be utterly noxious, fumes from these compounds.

I would mix up what seemed like half a ton of this stuff – but which never went half so far as you expected it to. I'd need to contort my hands and scrape the skin off my knuckles as I tried to press the sticky substance into the gap between the inner part of the door and the door panel, hoping against hope that it would seal them together – at least for a few more weeks.

It never did. Inevitably I would want to go out in the car before the thing was completely dry, and so I would close the door gingerly, hoping that the vibration wouldn't dislodge the sealant and thereby undo all of my efforts in a single clunk. All might be well for a day or two, but then the reasonably solid-sounding click of the door closing would give way to a rattle, and before I got to the next junction it was as though I hadn't bothered. But still, the following Saturday, we were out there again, on the pavement or in the garage, mixing up more and more of this evil gunk.

I must have got through tons of the stuff, but always it was fighting a losing battle.

So, anyway, I kept the VW Beetle for several years, man and boy, right up to the time I got my first proper job as a reporter for the BBC in the North East. By this time I was about 25 and earning fairly decent money, so I reckoned I could afford a new car.

At that point I don't think anyone in my family had ever owned a new car. Certainly my Dad hadn't and, if my brother had, he was now living a long way away and I had not been aware of it.

For some reason best known to myself, I fancied a Citroën. Maybe it was because I'd always loved those models that General De Gaulle used to ride around in. Big bullfrog-nosed things with hydro-pneumatic suspension. Equally, it could have been to do with the fact that Eric Robson owned one and it was marvellous.

Yes, that's right. It was the same Eric Robson – now probably most famous as the host of *Gardeners' Question Time* on Radio 4 but then, like me, a freelance TV reporter for BBC North East. At that time the BBC was housed in a former lying-in hospital in the centre of Newcastle. The building just about had space at the back to park six cars, but only if they parked close together in two rows of three. This meant that if the person driving the car in the middle wanted to get out, one of the cars in front or behind had to move, thus providing a constant source of irritation for all concerned.

Anyway, Eric had one of those huge great Citroën estate cars, which was about 30 percent longer than the average car, and therefore served to exacerbate the already tight-squeeze in the tiny car park. One day he offered to give me a lift to a job we were both covering, but before we could set off we had to wait for someone to move a car in front of us. While we were waiting Eric started the engine, and I remember being absolutely amazed and impressed that the car seemed to be taking a big intake of breath, and the whole thing lifted up several inches on its suspension.

My initial amazement was then overtaken by even greater amazement at the more extraordinary realisation that not only were we rising up in the air, but that the car in front of us was rising up in the air as well. He realised more quickly than I did that this meant that we were too close to it, and that the bumper of our car was underneath the bumper of that car, so we were having the effect of a fork-lift truck.

The problem now was that Eric couldn't reverse away without pulling the bumper off his own car or the car in front, or both. Then again he wasn't supposed to drive away before the suspension had done its thing.

Eventually we worked out that the only solution was to turn off the engine, allow our car to settle back down again, and then have the car in front drive away. It took us a little longer to work that out than it probably should have done, but we were both younger and more idiotic then than we are now. Probably.

Despite the obvious disadvantage that it would be absolutely useless as a getaway car, I still fancied the idea of a Citroën and was wondering what model to go for when one day I opened the *Sunday Times* colour supplement and saw it. There, across the two middle pages, was an awesome photograph of something called a Citroën Basalt. If I am honest, this car was just a fairly basic Citroën GS, but it did have an absolutely stunning paint job. All black, but with a series of parallel stripes down the side, of diminishing width, and in a sort of pinky red. And only now, writing this about 30 years later, does it occur to me that this paint job was fairly reminiscent of that sported by my first motoring love affair – with the Dinky toy of the Ford Thunderbird.

This thing was due to come out in a limited edition of 400. It had all the extras and gadgets and this very smart paint job, and I had to have one.

Maybe it is the filter of youth and the rosy glow of the first-ever new car, but to this day I still think that this was the prettiest car I ever owned. Everyone turned to look at it, and everyone who didn't know that Citroëns are fairly much a pile of crap admired it. Black cars always look smart, and this looked as smart as hell.

There is nothing quite like the smell of the interior of a brand-new car. Nothing quite like the utterly pristine carpets.

Nothing quite like seeing something like 000012 on the odometer. Nothing like the sheen of tyres straight out of the showroom, the deep shine of unblemished paintwork. Nothing quite like the little burst of joy you have as you drive it out of the garage, and see the admiring glances of anyone who notices a brand-new car.

You know the rest. I used to park my car outside the house we then occupied in Woodbine Road, and I had this new Citroën for about a week before I came out one morning and found the door had been kicked in. A great big dent in the passenger side, and the imprint of a size 12 boot on the smart red stripes. I was mortified. I looked at it in disbelief. My perfect new car now unmistakably blemished beyond recall.

My chagrin lasted for about five minutes before I found myself immensely relieved. How much of a prat was I, caring about what a car looked like? Since then I've always been relieved when I've got my first scratch or dent in a new car. It means that after that you can stop worrying about it, and not give a damn. So much more healthy – don't you think?

Mind you, if I could lay hands on the bastard who kicked the door in ...

8 All the old bollocks

Why is it, do you suppose, that for everything you want to do in life, no matter how apparently simple and uncontroversial, there seems to be an army of arseholes whose sole mission in life is to screw it up for you? Why should this be so?

These are people whose entire reason to be is to make life more difficult for the rest of us, and every member of these battalions of butt-heads seems to be impressively inventive in their ability to make up new bits of bollocks and bureaucracy to get in our way.

You could take anything as an example but, just by way of illustration and by way of a mildly diverting segue en route towards our real subject, let's take something as simple as wanting to get on an aeroplane.

All you actually want to do is to get on a plane. Here is a person. Here is a plane. I'd like to get on it and go somewhere. Looks simple enough? OK, so let's see what the squadrons of shit-for-brains have invented to make this apparently simple process more difficult.

First of all we need a ticket. OK, well that's probably fair enough, but how will we get one? Time was when you might pop down to the local travel agent. That was of course before the internet had put most of them out of business. If and when you do find a high street travel agent and pay a visit, you find yourself in a queue behind the couple who are booking the world cruise they have been promising themselves these last 25 years, with stops in Addis, Aden, Adelaide and Augusta, and that's before we get to the places they want to stop at beginning with B.

You could make a phone call, but that means negotiating the maze of recorded messages giving you a vast range of options you cannot comprehend, and listening to the entire cannon of the music of Vivaldi. Great composer, but blimey!

You could go on-line but the on-line booking system presumably makes sense to a 12-year-old but not to you.

Once you have found a way to book your ticket, no-one wants to hand it to you or to send it to you; nowadays you have to pick up an 'e-ticket' at the airport. Which means that you have to be able to read and accurately tap in a 16-digit code, making no error on pain of having to start the process all over again. Oh, and it's only at this point that you realise that you booked the ticket on a different credit card than the one you have brought with you.

You need a passport – which used to be a simple matter but is now a Kafkaesque labyrinth of bureaucracy and security checks. It's difficult enough for someone called John Bull who has lived here all his life; heaven help you if you have the word 'Hussein' somewhere in your name. Or indeed, anything that rhymes with Osama.

Once equipped with ticket and passport, there are 150

people ahead of you in the queue to check in, the same 150 ahead of you at airport security, and the same 150 ahead of you yet again as you try to get through passport control. And nowhere near enough people manning any of them.

So now – you need your passport, your ticket, your boarding card, all in different combinations to get through passport control, security, and the departure gate. You need your boarding card again if you want to buy anything from the duty-free, and your passport again if you want to buy some foreign currency. You have to take off your shoes and then put them on again. Watch, belt, wallet, cuff links, Stanley knife (oops, probably should have left that at home). When eventually you get on the plane you are required to sit strapped into a tiny seat for another 45 minutes, at imminent risk of death from frustration while they try to track down a passenger whose luggage is on the plane but whose arse isn't.

See what I mean? Entire platoons of plonkers getting in your face just because you want to do a simple thing like getting on a plane.

Same goes for trying to run a small business. Same goes for trying to open a bank account. Same goes for trying to rent or buy a house. Same old, same old, same old. In all of these cases, and so very many more, it seems to me that there are hundreds of horrible little people who all are desperate to insert their nasty little rules and regulations into whatever you are trying to do, and all are determined to find new and better ways to rip you off in the process.

OK, so the reason for rehearsing all this is that owning and driving a car has to be one of the worst of them. It's the 21st century, and if you want to do something as basic as motoring, just think about all of the bastards, in all of the different places,

who want to have a piece of you. All the stuff which, if you
didn't have to worry about it, could make your life so very much
more simple and straightforward. All the stuff which makes
ordinary people irritated, and which threatens to push Grumpy
Old Men and Grumpy Old Women – who are temperamen-
tally inclined to be irritated and hacked off even if nothing is
doing much to push them in that direction – metaphorically
and indeed physically over the precipice.

Actually, even as I sit here writing this I'm hyperventilat-
ing, and will do well to get to the end of the chapter without a
seizure, but let's have a go at it, shall we? Let's count the hurdles
between you and the driver's seat.

1   **You have to apply for a driving licence.**

2   **You have to take driving lessons.**

3   **You have to pass a driving test.**

4   **You have to go through extraordinary bollocks
    involved in buying a car.**

5   **You have to register as the owner.**

6   **You have to get the MOT.**

7   **You have to get insurance.**

8   **You have to get road tax.**

9   **You have to get it serviced.**

10 **You have to find somewhere to keep the car – which
    involves a whole new set of problems too extended to
    list here.**

... And none of that is to mention the Congestion Charge!

Originally it was my plan to go through the obstacles and complications and unnecessary crapulence involved in each of these in turn, itemising the various difficulties and frustrations involved in vaulting every hurdle on the assault course between you and freedom. However, I wasn't even halfway through describing the rigmarole of applying for a licence before I lost the will to live, and suspected that you would do the same.

Notwithstanding, I am going to take a little time out to talk about the process of buying a car in the first place. I have talked about this just a little bit before, but the reason I am returning to it is because, theoretically, this ought to be one of life's few pleasures for a Grumpy. The idea of selecting a new car should, it seems to me, be something to which even those of a quintessentially Grumpy disposition could look forward to. You know, the whole business of weighing up the merits of this versus that – the bigger engine versus the extra door at the back, the automatic or the gear lever. The number and location of the cup-holders. Real bloke stuff.

But it isn't. It really isn't.

As my mind wanders over the various times I've been in this position over the years, I'm trying to think of the common factor which makes all these experiences so loathsome, and I think I have it. I think it comes down to the essential and inescapable fact that Grumpy Old Men don't like to be pissed about. Or maybe it's not so much that we're being pissed about; it's more that we are being 'handled'.

These blokes (for it is always blokes) all come out of exactly the same mould. Sure, some are a bit up-market than others – maybe if they're trying to sell you a Mercedes rather than a Ford – but they're all basically the same sort of thing. What is it? Oily? No. They usually are, a bit, but that's not quite it. Manipulative? Yes, but still not exactly right. Not exactly. What is the word?

Oleaginous. I think that's it. They're oleaginous. I'm not sure that I've got the definition exactly right, but what the word means to me is 'a little bit creepy, but worse than just creepy they are handling us at the same time'. They have their spiel, which has been refined and practised and developed, and now is being put to work on us.

We're today's 'mark' and this bloke's commission depends on whether we are going to fall for it. Chances are that he's the showroom hotshot with a reputation to maintain. He's the bloke who, once he's got you in his sights, never lets you get away. And he is also the one famous among his colleagues at spotting the total nitwit who will go for the de luxe sports upgrade package, the extra protective valeting package and the extended warranty, whether the customer really wants them or not.

Well, I don't know what effect this has on you, and I guess it must work on a lot of people because otherwise presumably they would try something else. On me, and others who suffer from the Grumpy syndrome as severely as I do, it's torture.

I don't really want to go through all the bollocks of changing my car at all, but if I do have to go through it from time to time I'd like to be able to ask this bloke a few questions without getting a load of bloody eyewash for an answer. For example, I'd like to be able to ask him the trade-in value of my old car, without having to endure all the sucking of gums, the 'if only it had been the Mark 3 instead of the Mark 2', or the 'there's not much of a market for this model since the Mark 5 came out.'

I guess I can understand why they have to walk around my old car with a diagram of a car on their clipboard, putting a cross on the page anywhere there is a blemish. I can imagine why they have to record and thereby remind you of the time you parked too close to the pavement and scuffed the hubcap. I suppose I realise why they have to sit themselves in the driving seat and check that what I've said about the mileage is true.

Yes, I guess I can understand why they have to do all these things, but I hate it all the same.

Don't you? Suddenly, when this begins to happen, I find that the car I haven't given a bugger about these last three years starts to bring out a new emotion in me. I feel protective towards it. Like a child you were thinking of putting up for adoption. Just right about now, and for no reason I can explain, I feel myself resenting the hand brushing over the upholstery to see how worn it is, and the lifting of the bonnet lid to see whether it's ever been opened before.

Then the bloke always asks you if you can 'bear with me for a minute' because he has to confer with his boss. You'll see him go into a little office with a glass wall, and try to get the attention of some oily git who looks like him but is just a little bit slicker. Just a little bit older. Just a little bit more of a total head-louse. You see them both glance over at you as they discuss whether they think you are a total prat who can be taken for the full ride, and what's most irritating of all is that you suspect that they do.

At last he'll leave the office, come over to you and say that he just needs to check something else, and then he'll go into his routine.

'If we can come to an agreement, are you ready to do a deal today?'

At this point I always just want to say 'get stuffed', but I seldom do. Instead I fall in with the game and admit that, yes, if we can agree terms, we can do a deal today.

Then sometimes he'll ask you what you think your car is worth. This is because, if you are an idiot, there is at least a chance that you'll say a number which is lower than he has in his mind. In that case he'll still umm, and aah, but he'll reluctantly agree to your price. When they ask me that question I always add about £3,000 to the price I am really thinking of, just to try to spoil their day.

'Well the book price for a car in the condition of yours is ...' and then he'll say a number that is always going to be at least £1,500 lower than you were hoping. 'But', he'll say, 'we would like to do business with you today, so my boss has said we can make an exception and do a deal on the price of the car you are buying ...' (This is assuming of course that you are going for the sporty de luxe upgrade, etc, etc, which has already added £3,000 to the price.)

So now he wants you to lose sight of the question of how much you are going to get for your old car, and he wants you to lose sight of how much you are paying for your new car. At this point he wants to start talking about the 'cost of change'.

'If the cost of change was going to be £7,000, how would that sound to you?'

'That would sound to me like a bloody outrage,' is what I always say, or some small variation on the theme. 'That would sound like I ought to be calling the police because, though you don't seem to have a mask and a gun, this is as near to a mugging as I can recall.'

When I say that, he usually doesn't know what to make of it, and you see that look spreading over his face. Suddenly he's outside the usual script and in unknown territory. Is he dealing with a wise-arse, or a lunatic? Maybe you are a gullible idiot, but maybe not. He needs to go back and confer again with his boss to see if they can go even further outside their usual limits of generosity ...

So I won't labour the point very much further, but I've gone this far just to illustrate what a stupid bloody game it all is. How something, which would be bad enough if it was just straightforward, inevitably turns into a little jousting match with someone you'd usually wade through manure to avoid

even speaking to, let alone doing business with. How buying a new car – a routine and possibly even enjoyable thing for a normal person – becomes part of the everyday agony involved with being a Grumpy.

And that is not to mention all the other old bollocks which is attendant on every other aspect of buying, owning and running a car. An apparently simple thing made inordinately complex and irredeemably awful by fuck-wits. Such is the Grumpy's lot. If you are one, you'll recognise the syndrome, and perhaps take comfort from the idea that you are not alone. And if you aren't one, you'll probably wonder what on earth I am talking about.

So whereas the good news about cars and driving may once have been the open road, the wind in your hair, the freedom to come and go as you pleased, the bad news is that – like so many other aspects of everyday life – the wart-brains have got hold of it and made it yet another excuse for pissing us about. Cluttering up our lives with forms to complete and rules to observe and payments to be made here and payments to be made there. All the old bollocks – in fact – which makes Grumpies grumpy. As hell.

9 The Happy Puker

Does anyone remember the Happy Puker?

I think it was properly known as the Happy Eater, and was a chain of roadside cafés, the memorable thing about which was the logo. Remember? It involved a circular cartoon head of someone with a very large mouth, sticking their index finger down their throat.

I am sure this logo must have seemed a great idea when it was first designed, but then gradually, as the particular gesture became an unmistakable symbol for a person throwing up, it seemed more and more unfortunate. In our family we never knew it as anything other than 'the Happy Puker' which then became our soubriquet for the whole gamut of motorway service stations or restaurants-on-a-roundabout. I believe the name and logo were changed when the Happy Puker was taken over. The sentiment changed but the substance remained the same.

If anyone ever wanted a perfect illustration of the virtues of free-market competition, you would only have to wheel out the example of motorway service stations. In a nutshell, the structure of the motorway system means that you cannot have a free-for-all. Having roadside cafés in lay-bys, as they do on so many A-roads, would simply not be practical on a motorway, and so there is an opportunity – approximately 1 in every 25 miles – to provide a stopping-off point for petrol, refreshments and a wee. It's an opportunity that commercial companies have to bid for but, once they've got it, it's open season. They effectively have you over a barrel.

Of course you could drive off the motorway for miles and miles and miles trying to find another petrol station that is open, or maybe a roadside café, but the truth is that all you want to do is to get this motorway-driving hell behind you as quickly as possible. It's more or less inevitable, therefore, that you are going to stop to refuel yourself and your car at a motorway service station.

So what are these places like? Really. What are they bloody well like?

Usually I'll do almost anything conceivable to avoid having to actually buy something to eat at a motorway service station. It's not so much that I mind being mugged in broad daylight; that seems to happen all the time. What I object to is being forced to pay about four times what something should normally cost, and then also have it be shit. Do you know what I mean?

I remember once stopping at a Granada Service Station – and I remember that it was Granada because I worked for Granada TV at the time – and queuing to buy a burger. God knows what I must have been thinking of – maybe I was feeling suicidal or reckless or just out of it – but anyway I found myself at the back of this queue of about ten people standing at the counter.

There was only one person serving and she, God bless her, was plainly someone who was mentally challenged in some way. I know it doesn't reflect well on me to have observed this, or to point it out, but I need to give you the full picture of this experience. Putting this girl in sole charge of this establishment was plainly way outside her abilities, and the poor kid not only had to take the orders and serve the food, but also had to make the tea or coffee, take the money and give the change as well. And there was a queue; a queue of people who had just been driving 20 miles per hour faster than the speed limit because they are in a hurry to get to their destination, and are now having to waste the time they have thereby saved by standing in this queue.

Eventually, after what must have been about ten minutes but felt like ten years, I got to the counter and ordered a cheeseburger. I didn't 'want fries with it' and I didn't want a drink with it. I just wanted the cheeseburger.

'How much is that please?'

'That'll be £4.50.'

No really. It was £4.50, which I would have thought was a bit on the toppy side even if it had been edible. As it was, the resemblance of the object served to a cheeseburger was approximately the same as the relationship between an interview with John McCrirrick and a piece of entertainment. Or an earwig to a giraffe. Or a pile of stale horse-dung to Darcy Bussell. I think maybe you get the idea. It was not a cheeseburger in the conventional understanding of the term.

But the point of course was that there was nowhere else to go. Obviously you could say 'sod it, I'm not putting up with this,' but then the alternative was to go hungry, because this was the only eating place for 25 miles, and the next eating place

Motorway Service Area

The term 'service' in this context lies entirely within the realm of the operator's imagination and any similarity with the dictionary definition is purely coincidental (and probably a sacking offence)

25 miles up the road was likely to be every bit as bad, or worse.

They've got you – so they put together the worst possible food, with the lowest common denominator service, and the highest possible prices – and you have to like it or lump it. Personally, these days, I always lump it. I fill up my car with fuel at a service station as close as I can to the start of the motorway, and then I don't stop until I'm off it again. Occasionally I have to stop to take a leak – which seems to me to be about the only appropriate thing to do in one of these places.

I'm not going to go into all the horrors involved in motorway service stations. They're run as only a monopoly can be run, and the least said about them the better. The only observation I simply cannot resist making is about the amusements. How priceless is it, do you think, to see the bloody idiots who've just got out of the Ford Cosworth or the souped-up Astra, sitting on a 'Le Mans 24-hour race' driving machine? It's almost worth paying for the entertainment.

So I'll leave this little section by retailing a little anecdote which I heard so often when I worked at Granada that I genuinely believe it is true. It involves one of the founding brothers of the company, Sydney Bernstein.

When the business was first set up, Sydney apparently had the habit of stalking the corridors of any and all of his establishments, bursting open any closed door without warning and demanding to know what the person inside was doing. The person thus accosted was obliged to give a full account of themselves, and in particular how they were spending Sydney's money.

All things considered, the Bernsteins were very benign employers, but this little foible did have the effect of striking fear into middle managers in particular.

One day, quite unannounced, Sydney ordered his driver to pull into a motorway service station and, without alerting anyone to what he was doing, he headed for the kitchens. He burst through the doors and proceeded to march around, wiping his finger over dusty surfaces, observing food in corridors waiting to be cooked, and demanding to know what the people he came across were doing.

After a little while the site manager was alerted and hurried to the spot where Sydney was continuing his inspection. The manager followed along in the wake of Sydney's hurricane, and was required to note down an extensive list of criticisms and observations. Eventually the procession came to a halt at the door of Sydney's car.

'Have you got all that?' Sydney enquired.

'Yes sir, I think I have,' said the manager. 'But may I ask a question?'

'And what might that be?'

'May I ask who exactly are you?'

'I am Sydney Bernstein, and I am the chairman of the Granada Group.'

The site manager is reported not to have missed a beat.

'Well it's very kind of you to point out all these things and I'm sure we'll see to them. But there is just one thing that perhaps you should be aware of.'

'And what's that?'

'This isn't one of your service stations.'

10 Little princess on board

Despite what the lay person might suspect, Grumpy Old Men and Grumpy Old Women don't actively go around the place looking for things to get annoyed about. We don't. Believe it or not, wherever possible we try to let stuff that has every potential to get up the collective snitch to go past us. But honestly ... some things seem positively to have been designed to irritate, and any kind of sticker in a car window falls into the category.

Personally I could never understand why anyone would allow the garage you bought the car from to use you as a touring billboard for their business, displaying an advertisement with their name and address in your rear window. These businesses have almost always ripped you off in one way or another, so why on earth would you give them a free plug for their trouble?

Over the years I have had hours of fun and broken fingernails trying to remove these stickers and then all trace of them from the windows of cars I've owned. Eventually, of course, you get to the point where your indolence overtakes your irritation, and so the sticker stays there. Or anyway, they've given you no choice by making it an indelible part of the registration plate, or stuck it on the tax disc, or something.

Does anyone remember those multi-coloured plastic flags we had when we were kids which indicated which coastal resorts we had visited, and which obscured visibility out of most of the windows in your Dad's car? Not much to object to there, I don't suppose, which may be the reason that they seem to have been only a passing fad.

Then there was a fashion for those long white stickers which said terribly witty things like 'Don't follow me, I'm lost'. Anyone remember that? As kids we always thought these were hilarious, and could never understand why our Mum and Dad would not acquiesce to our repeated attempts to persuade them to buy and display one. I think I get it now.

I remember another side-splitter which had an arrow pointing to the right which said 'over-taker' and another one pointing to the inside lane labelled 'undertaker.' I guess it might be from things like this that I first got my love of language.

Obviously the example that is guaranteed to make any serious Grumpy tut and blow and look skywards is the now notorious 'Baby on Board'. Once, when I was going on in what I must have thought was an hilarious manner about what a pain this was, someone told me that these were first invented by the fire department in a big American city to inform emergency workers going to a wreck that they should also look for a little mite in the carnage. When I heard that I must admit that I felt a very slight pang of guilt about always having been so cynical and nasty about them. But this passed very quickly, and now they provide me with as potent a source of irritation as ever they did. Indeed, seeing one induces a Pavlovian response in which my foot goes down hard on the accelerator.

'Baby on Board'. What are we supposed to make of that? That this car is being driven by a smug little couple who are fertile. Oh yes, look at us. We've got genes that are so very powerful that just one glance at her from me and she was pregnant. So we have had a baby. We are the first and only people in the world to have performed this miracle, and it is in the car with us right now, so you had better watch it. Yes that's right, if you had been thinking of driving too close, or maybe giving us a quick nudge forwards at the next set of traffic lights, then you can just think again. We've got a 'baby on board' so we need an invisible force-field around us. Our precious little bundle of humanity is so important, so fragile, such a gift to the world that everyone else has to know about it and give us a wide berth (oh dear).

I remember in the first series of *Grumpy Old Men* that Tony Hawks wanted to know what happened when the baby was *not* on board. Did the sticker come down? Was it replaced with 'Baby staying with grandma for a day or two'? Or 'Baby being looked after by the Filipina'? Where is the baby? We need to know where this bloody baby is.

All that was bad enough, but nothing that is just irritating can be left merely to irritate. Someone somewhere always has to ramp it up, so that before we knew where we were, we were being treated to 'Little person on board'. Or 'Very important little person on board'. 'Little princess on board'. For heaven's sake! Have these people no shame whatsoever?

And if you get stuck alongside these people at the traffic lights and you glance into their back seat, inevitably you can instantly see that it is indeed a little princess on board. A horrible, spotty, overweight, over-indulged horror of a little princess who probably skweemed and skweemed and skweemed until daddy agreed to put the bloody stupid sticker in the window.

Personally I was just desperate to find the sticker which said 'What does it matter who the fuck is on board?' but I never did. Probably just as well. It would only have led to altercations.

Still more recently, I think, but every bit as bloody vexing to me and other Grumpies of my ilk is the sign which says 'How am I driving? – phone ...' and then gives a phone number. Does anyone really know what is going on here?

When I first saw one of these I assumed that they must have been introduced by the owners of fleets of vehicles, as a way of trying to ensure that their drivers weren't driving around like lunatics. I guessed that the idea must be that when one of these white-van-men cuts you up at the traffic lights you see the sign on the back of his vehicle, phone the number on the sticker and grass him up to his boss.

Has anyone ever done this? Have any of your friends ever done this? Has anyone you know ever done this? I don't think so. I think that most of us think that if you did this you would get through to a recorded message. Or you would find yourself with a 'choice of options'. Or you will get through to an oik in a factory somewhere in the Black Country where someone with an accent you can't understand won't give a damn.

Worse still – he *will* give a damn, but will want to take your name and address and details, and then the driver will be fired, will come round to your house, burst his way in through the front door, and leave you lying a bleeding mess on the carpet. Or have I been watching too much telly?

More recently I had an idea that I'd like to stick one of these notices on my car, and give my own mobile number. Then, if anyone calls to complain to someone they think is my boss about my driving, I can say 'yes, and I'm driving right in front of you now,' and will get out at the next lights and fill him in. However, that's the sort of thing I occasionally think about doing, but never really would. Maybe when I was younger, but certainly not now.

Anyway none of that matters, because I don't think any of us ever rings the number on the sticker. Just like we never bothered to ring the number on the 'cones hotline'. Remember that? It was the only initiative ever taken by John Major in the whole of his PMship. The idea was that, if we found ourselves on a Bank Holiday sitting in a traffic queue while two lanes were coned off and no-one was working, we could ring the 'cones hotline' and tell whoever answered the phone. Quite what they would do about it, thus making your plight easier, remained unstated. So I'm guessing that no-one bothered, and eventually it was quietly abandoned. Not unlike John Major, in fact.

No, 'how am I driving?' is just more imported-from-America bollocks which we could do without. Having said which, there is one very American tradition that I am sorry to say has not caught on in this country, and that is the bumper sticker. I used to travel back and forth to the USA quite a lot, and came to enjoy these little items as a minor art form.

What's appealing about bumper stickers is that they tend, in the first instance, to start out fairly straightforward, as in 'Vote Bush'. But then after a short while there is often a witty response, almost like a freeway conversation. For example in my book 'Re-defeat George Bush' takes some beating. And then this itself develops into what can be a healthy line in political banter of the 'Somewhere in Texas there's a village missing an idiot' variety.

Bumper stickers also seem to have an irresistible appeal

to religious nuts, so you get a lot of 'Jesus is my co-pilot'. But then again, in the land of the First Amendment where comment is free even if you piss off your neighbour, you get the healthy rejoinder 'Jesus was my co-pilot, but we crashed into a mountain and I had to eat him'. Similarly 'Jesus loves you' was quickly complemented by 'Jesus loves you. Everyone else thinks you're an asshole'.

My all-time favourite, which I picked up on a trip to the US about 20 years ago and brought back to display on my car at home simply said 'Shit Happens'. This seemed to me to be such a neat summary of life in general, and life on the road in particular, that I temporarily found it irresistible.

I also think we miss an opportunity to break the monotony of driving by not adopting the American habit of printing the slogan of the state of origin on the registration plate. Most famously, of course, this is 'Florida: The Sunshine State'

Or 'California: The Botox State'. With that special brand of humour, which the Americans seem to be especially good at, goddamn it, they've come up with a whole arsenal of stuff to amuse and entertain as you sit in gridlock on the 8-lane freeway.

'Arizona: But It's A Dry Heat' is a good one. 'Kentucky: Five Million People; Fifteen Last Names' delightfully self-deprecating. Or my personal favourite, 'Ohio: At Least We're Not Michigan'.

Wouldn't it make the day less irksome if we in Britain could adopt some of this highway banter? We try, of course, but in our very English way, with those ridiculous slogans that adorn so many county road signs. I think it was Sir Tim Rice, in one of our Grumpy series, who pointed out the absurdity of 'Berkshire: County on the Move'. County on the move? Where is it going to be when I come back?

A glance at the internet quickly reveals a whole selection of still less appealing county slogans. Take for example some imaginative and joyful little treasures like:

Clackmannanshire: 'The Wee County'

Or the slightly less pithy ...

Kirkcudbright: 'Scenic fishing town with an artistic heritage'

For those who couldn't quite make up their minds there is:

Tweeddale: 'Adventure, activity, culture, tranquillity'

What no hookers? No, for that we have to go to:

Dumfries and Galloway: 'A touch of the exotic'

Only a very slight touch of the exotic, mark you, but a touch nevertheless. Then there is:

Yorkshire: 'Alive with Opportunity!'

Which just means that they'd rather you think about opportunity when you arrive at the borders of their county than what you are actually thinking about ... 'the Ripper'.

Lincolnshire: 'Big County, Big Skies, Big Future'

Hey, the past has been shit, so the future can only be better. Then there is the completely unforgivable, such as:

Derbyshire and Peak District: 'Take a peak'

Shropshire: 'Love from Shropshire'

Mid-Wales: 'Because mid-Wales is as unique as you are'

Pembrokeshire: 'Wales [sic] most popular coastal destination'

And probably worst of all:

London: 'Totally LondON' whatever the hell that means.

So all these seem to me like a total failure of imagination, and a lost opportunity to amuse and entertain the motorist as he or she tries to get through your dreadful county as quickly as possible. Can you imagine how much more fun it would be if they said things like:

Cumbria: 'Go home a little bit more radioactive'

Or

Grimsby: 'A lot nicer than it sounds'

Or

'We know who put the T in Britain, but who put the cunt in Scunthorpe?'

OK, well maybe not.

But while we're on the subject of signs, what are you going to make of that little line that they write on the bottom of the wing mirror of some cars – OBJECTS IN THE MIRROR ARE CLOSER THAN THEY APPEAR. Really – what are you going to make of that? Can I be the only one who most definitely wants objects in the mirror to be exactly as close as they appear? Surely it can't be just me who wants to know that the cyclist I can see coming up on the outside is right next to me rather than 20 yards back? 'Objects are closer than they appear?' MAKE THEM THE SAME DISTANCE AS THEY APPEAR!

But I've left 'til last the worst, the very worst and most nauseating aspect of stickers and signs when you are out driving, and that is of course the slogans on the back of trade vehicles. I'm going to spare you the whole litany, because you know the sort of thing favoured especially, it seems, by plumbers. Instead, I'm going to go right to the one I saw just about a week ago and which, for me, perfectly exemplifies what makes Grumpy Old Men and Grumpy Old Women grumpy.

What is it?

Ocado – the people who deliver groceries for Waitrose and maybe for all I know, others. On the back of their vans it says 'DELIVERED WITH DEVOTION'.

Delivered with devotion? Delivered with devotion? What on earth can that possibly mean?

Left up to myself I might choose a whole range of things to have delivered with my groceries. I might like to have them delivered with, or by, a strippagram. I might like to have them delivered with a complimentary bunch of spring onions. I might like to have them delivered with a nice little bottle of Beaujolais.

But, in the real world, what I would really like from Ocado is that they delivered the stuff that I ordered, sometimes within about an hour of the time they said they were going to deliver it.

And that's all any of us want. We don't want our groceries 'delivered with devotion' – we don't even know what that means, and we only know that it alliterates, and that if 'delivered' had started with a P, the sign would have read 'delivered with passion' – which is probably what they do at Pret a Manger.

No. Groceries delivered by Ocado on behalf of Waitrose may or may not be delivered on time, they may or may not include the stuff you ordered, and you may or may not pay a ton of money for the privilege of being jerked about. But, on the other hand, they are 'delivered with devotion'.

So that's it. I'm officially lost for words.

11 Advanced Grumpiness

Have you ever thought about taking the test for Advanced Motorists?

In common with other men not afflicted by Grumpiness, most Grumpy Old Men think of themselves as pretty good drivers. We certainly think that with all of our experience and worldly wisdom we would be able to cruise through something like an Advanced Motorist's Test.

Of course, in reality most Grumpy Old Men are also too grumpy and basically indolent to be bothered actually to do anything about it. And, indeed, lurking somewhere not very far beneath the surface is the thought of the personal ignominy which would be consequent in the event that one might decide to take such a test, and then should do anything other than sail through with flying colours.

Anyway, the notion of taking this test is something that has been floating somewhere around the back of my mind for years and years. Ordinarily, by this stage in my life the idea would have been consigned to the ever-expanding 'stuff I'll probably never get round to' bin. You know, along with things like releasing a hit record, learning to fly a helicopter or swimming the Channel. Ordinarily that would be that, but then more recently I had a brief conversation with a policeman who told me that I could get a significant discount off my insurance premium, so I started thinking about actually doing it.

I don't know whether this is true, but I once heard that one of the things you have to do on the Advanced Motorist's test is to provide a running commentary for the examiner about the road ahead. You drive along, presumably with him in the passenger seat, and chat away to demonstrate your powers of anticipation. For example, you tell him well in advance if you are seeing a pedestrian with a woolly hat and an iPod who looks as though he could be about to cross the road. Or that you have spotted a driver who is texting his girlfriend and whose car is consequently veering dangerously into the path of the oncoming traffic. You know the sort of thing.

Partly by way of half-hearted practice against the prospect of actually going in for this test, and partly as a way of alleviating the ever-present boredom, I began to find myself providing this running commentary in my head. However, what I found was that this particular running commentary is so similar in style and substance to the one that runs through my head involuntarily while driving anyway, that I feel sure that I would not be able to trust myself to differentiate the two if actually in test conditions.

If you are one of us, you've done this yourself. It goes something like this.

'Now I wonder which one of these wankers is going to pause for just a second to let me pull out? They can all see that

I'm indicating, and the traffic is moving at the pace of the three-legged sloth, so what difference could it make? Will it be you? No. You're too much of a dick-head. Will it be you? Obviously not – you're too busy filling out your sales report. Oh thank you madam, at last someone with some common sense. A quick wave. Oh that's a nice smile ... I wonder if ...? No, don't be silly, she's just being pleasant. Now what's that bloke doing? Oh, good idea, just indicate and pull out straight into the traffic. Poor bastard ahead has to swerve to avoid him. This hold-up is worse than usual. I wonder what the hell that's about. Maybe more road works ahead. Blimey, this road has had more trenches in it in the last year than the Maginot Line. Oh good, the traffic lights aren't working again – which would be fine except that they've put some prat in a uniform at the junction and he's letting more people go across than he's letting go through. What an idiot. Maybe I'll blast my horn. No, that'll probably make it worse.'

As you can no doubt tell, I could go on and on and on like this. Indeed, I do go on and on like this. On and on and on. In my mind. And I think you do too. I think that as we look around us, at everyone else who is stuck in the same utterly insane lines of cars, feeling our lives tick past, our hearts beating beats that they will never beat again, we are all thinking the same thing. Something along the lines of – 'wouldn't it be great if there were about one-third of the number of people in the world that there are. Then maybe those who were left would be able to live a civilised life.'

So that's that then. None of us Grumpies could trust ourselves to take a test like the Advanced Motorist's, because we know in our hearts that before very long our calm and patient 'I see a chap waiting at the next junction and am ready to brake because I anticipate that he might pull out without waiting for a sufficient gap,' would become 'look at that arsehole in the white van who can't wait to barge his way into the traffic. Bastard. If he thinks he's getting in front of me he can go and fuck himself.' Which probably isn't what they're looking for.

So that's another way in which Grumpies are persecuted. We can't qualify for reduced motoring insurance.

Meanwhile, on a related subject, do you find yourself doing a constant mental audit of the cars you are overtaking on the motorway, versus the cars overtaking you?

I fear I may be going somewhat out on a limb here, because I have an uncomfortable feeling that I may be alone or in a very small group of eccentrics who do this. However, this is no time to start worrying about all that sort of stuff, so here goes.

I'm guessing that we're all familiar with that feeling of driving along in the outside lane, doing maybe 80 or so, and glancing up to see a huge shiny Porsche or Ferrari coming up in your rear-view mirror like a fast-approaching hound of hell, and all but barging you out the way. It doesn't have to be a sports car – sometimes it can be a big BMW or Mercedes or Bentley. Something big and fast and taking no prisoners.

When that happens to me my instinct is to get out of the way quickly to let them past. I know this isn't everyone's instinct. I know there are plenty of people who sit and think 'I'm already exceeding the speed limit, which means that he must be exceeding it by even more, so I am going to sit here and let him wait.'

I'm not one of those people. When this happens to me, something goes off in my head along the lines of 'he's driving a big new powerful fuck-off car; I'm driving my fairly modest runabout. It's my job to get out of his way and to let him through.' In a split second it seems that I have done a mental calculation of what he's spent on his car, versus what I've spent on my car, and I'm sort of thinking that it's OK for him to overtake me. He's paid for it.

Something similar goes on when I am overtaking someone else. If I am in the fast lane and going quicker than the car I am coming up behind, I'm doing an unconscious calculation about whether or not he is entitled to be in front of me, or whether by rights I should be in front of him. Is his car older than mine? Less powerful than mine? Crappier than mine?

If the answer to these is 'yes' then I feel he should be getting out of my way.

Meanwhile, if an old or nasty-looking car overtakes me on the motorway, I'm usually wondering at some level who he thinks he is. Similarly, if I overtake a car that's obviously newer, more expensive and more powerful than mine, in some way I feel I've got one over on him. OK, so is all this nuts, or does it ring a bell with you? I just haven't got a clue.

It may be that you are thinking 'he's barmy' and congratulating yourself that you don't have these trivial and petty-fogging thoughts as you eat up the miles. On the other hand, if you are feeling supercilious, just try to remember what you feel when you find yourself being overtaken by a Smart car. Eh? Have I got you? Don't you in some way think 'bloody cheek – in a car like that he shouldn't be exceeding 30'? I'll bet you do.

So anyway, for better or for worse, it's out there. I'm a bit potty. If I go to work on the day of publication and find a couple of men greeting me wearing white coats and speaking in soothing voices, I'll know that fessing up to this was a mistake. If not, maybe we're all as deranged as one another.

12 Why?

How is it, do you suppose, that we are all willing to put up with it?

I'm serious – just think about it for a minute. Just think about all of the collected irritations, delays and difficulties which are caused to our daily lives by the fact that it's more or less impossible to get around by road. Just think about how more or less anything and everything we do, for more or less every waking hour of every day, is dictated in some way or another by the exigencies involved in getting around in a car.

Once you start thinking about it, it's amazing that there isn't a spontaneous uprising every bloody day of the year. That people don't take to the streets and start breaking things up. Who is supposed to be organising this mess? And how have they managed to stay off the guillotine?

Let's just take one or two examples of the traffic-related stuff that is so irritating and so commonplace that it threatens civil disorder.

First of all, there is no reliable way of predicting how much time it will take you to accomplish any journey you want to take in a big town or city. Think about it. There is no way on earth of knowing whether a journey of six miles across town, which should take maybe 20 minutes, is going to take 20 minutes, or 2 hours. No way to know.

We live in south-west London and, since the public transport system seems to have been designed as though our house was at some time the epicentre of an appalling Chernobyl-style accident, we frequently have to drive in and out of central London in the car.

Now I swear to God that if I leave an hour and a half to travel the six miles to Waterloo Bridge, it'll take 25 minutes. If I leave 45 minutes, it'll take 90. So fragile, and so pathetic, is the system of roads in what we're often told is the greatest capital city in the world that the most trivial incident, caused by the most otherwise inconsequential person, trying to do an utterly uncontroversial thing, will cause absolute bloody mayhem.

How often have you sat there, at the back of what seems to be an unending queue of cars, nudging and inching forward, for minute upon minute, maybe even hour upon hour, and when you eventually get to the cause of the hold-up, it's a bloke with a flat tyre, or a tiny scrape between a woman in a 4 × 4 and a white-van man. Or whatever. And this has disrupted your journey, and the journey of the bloke in front, and the person behind, and the person in front and behind of them, for mile after mile after mile.

Often it seems as though a whole sector of the city has ground to a halt because someone you've never met, somewhere you have never been, has had a minor altercation with a traffic island. It's the roadside equivalent of the butterfly in South America causing the tsunami in Japan, or whatever it is. A broken windscreen wiper in Wolverhampton causes gridlock in Galashiels.

And the other thing is that when you get to the front of the queue, no-one involved in the incident seems remotely interested in, or concerned about, the mayhem they are causing to half the population. Usually the offending car has been pushed off the carriageway onto the verge or pavement, and the driver is sitting on the side of the road, presumably waiting for a tow-truck, and the only thing obstructing the traffic is a set of rubber road cones which are still there for no apparent reason but are blocking off an entire lane.

Sometimes there will be a policeman present, and he or she doesn't seem to give a bugger either. You feel like winding the window down as you go by and saying 'does anyone here have the slightest notion whatsoever that you are causing a tailback which goes as far back as bloody Guildford?' But the truth is that you are now so relieved to have at last got to the front of the queue that you don't really give a stuff about the people behind you either, so you just tuck it away in the 'another sodding irritation' bank and get on your way. But really.

Most often, when we're trying to get into town, it's because we're going to something in the evening where we more or less have to arrive on time. Or you're going to miss the first act. Or the first course. Or the queue is going to be too long.

The truth is that, being of an uncompromisingly Grumpy persuasion generally, I'm usually in a bad mood about this before I start. There are very few things that seem to me to be worth all the effort of schlepping through the commuter traffic into the centre of London in the evening.

However, on the odd occasion – such as maybe when Eric is appearing at the Royal Albert Hall, or ... well, I'm already

stumped for something else that's worth it. Anyway, on the odd occasion that it's worth the trouble, I want to be sure to arrive in good time, so I err on the side of caution. I set off early, except that this usually means that I am so early that I cross the boundary of the congestion charge just a few minutes before 6.00 and have to pay £8. Or more often I forget about it and have to pay a fine of £50. Unless I delay paying the fine in which case it's a fine of £100.

That done, I am in town 45 minutes before I need to be, and so I have to find somewhere where it's possible to sit in the car and wait. If and when I do find somewhere to put the car, it's usually about half a mile from the place I eventually want to get to. Sometimes I'll find a parking meter, but it's about 20 past 6, and I'm buggered if I want to put £1 in the machine just to get me through this last ten minutes before I don't need to pay. It's not that I am especially mean – though maybe I am – it's more that having already paid £8 to get into London, somehow that last £1 for ten minutes on a meter feels like the thing that is going to send me over the edge.

So I sit in the car, scanning all the mirrors in every direction, to ensure that no traffic warden will pounce and have his bloody ticket half-written before I get the chance to leap out and remonstrate.

'I was just going to put some money in the meter.'

'I've been watching you for ten minutes.'

If I'm absolutely honest, precisely this has never happened to me, but it's the anticipation of this kind of debacle that obsesses me at the beginning of what should otherwise be a pleasant evening.

OK, so now forget about the journeys that are unpredictable, and think about the ones that *are* predictable. Take a look at the M25 on a Friday night. I just chose Friday night to make my point, but actually you can choose any night, or any morning. Or the M4, or the M62 over the Pennines, or the A19 between Newcastle and Sunderland, or the M6, or the M27 going west from Southampton. In fact, take more or less any road anywhere in the bloody country at almost any time of the day or night, and you'll see people queuing in traffic jams.

Sitting in their insulated armchairs for hour after hour after hour, waiting, waiting, waiting. Their heartbeats ticking away, their lives trickling by, seconds and minutes and hours that they can never get back again. Totally wasted time – hours upon hours upon hours of futility. Tick tick tick tick tick.

All of these people, in all of these cars, and just sitting there, waiting to get somewhere else. There can be little or no useful activity – we're just biding our time 'til this airhead in front of us decides to move, or maybe it's the airhead in front of him, or the one in front of him, etc, etc. Quite possibly at the front of this queue a new driver has stalled the engine at the traffic lights, and the dick-head behind her thinks it will be helpful to give her a toot on the horn. (Why do people do that, by the way?) This of course has had the effect of making her stall again, so what might have been a hesitation becomes a hiatus, and what might have been a hiatus becomes a hold-up.

So what are we going to do while we wait? Maybe we're going to listen to something improving on the radio? Use the opportunity to learn a new language? Mug up on our Shake-speare? Enjoy a talking book from the Grumpy range? More probably we are going to listen to some mindless tosh being warbled by a dimwit from one of the countless dimwits who somehow get away with it on local radio stations up and down the land.

Maybe instead we're going to be listening to some music. A little Wagner perhaps to get us in a suitably aggressive mood to do battle for the last parking space when we eventually get there. The Ride of the Valkyries is always an appropriate overture to an assault on any metropolis. The smell of napalm in the morning, and all that stuff.

Just for a moment, leave aside the human cost in terms of stress, angst, lost time, lost opportunity. Forget about that for a moment and just think of the economic cost of it.

I live just off the A3 going into London from the south-west, and most often when I go to work in the mornings the traffic is queuing back two or three miles from the end of the dual carriageway. Sometimes it will be worse than that, and when it is worse than that it's usually because they have been doing some work on the carriageway over the weekend, have not finished on schedule, and have left a lane closed off with their bits of debris on the other side of a long row of rubber road cones.

When that happens – as trivial a cause for delay as I can think of – it adds at least another 15 minutes on the journey time of every person, in every car, going along that route that day. I don't know how many cars that involves, but let's say it's 10,000. I don't think it can be any less. Maybe 1 in 4 cars has more than one person in it, so that's 12,500 lots of 15 minutes which that row of cones has taken out of all those people's day.

Since they are commuting into London during the rush hour, it's probably fair to assume that the people in these cars are earning more than the minimum wage, so for the sake of argument let's say they would be making £8 an hour. It's probably a lot more, but let's be conservative so as not to overstate the point.

In order to pay someone £8 an hour, an employer probably has to make income from that work of at least £12 an hour. So we're looking at 12,500 multiplied by £12 and then divided by 4 (4 lots of 15 minutes in an hour), which equals £37,500.

So that little row of rubber road cones, which maybe could have been cleared away last night, but instead has caused a 15-minute delay to motorists using the dual carriageway this morning, has cost £37,500 in lost working time and money. Theoretically.

One little hold-up, on one little road, on one little morning.

Obviously there are lots of variables in my calculations. I may be wrong in the number of cars. Or maybe about the amount those delayed would have earned, or maybe if they hadn't been waiting they wouldn't have been working. But let's say I'm wrong by a factor of 100%. Let's say I'm wrong by a factor of 200%. Even if I am wrong by a factor of 500%, we are still talking about millions upon millions upon millions of pounds in lost earning power every day, just because no-one involved with looking after the free flow of traffic on Britain's roads could give a damn. About you. About me. About any amount of inconvenience, mayhem, cost, delay or outrage.

Obviously, like all Grumpy Old Men who spout on about this and that, I know absolutely bugger all about traffic, traffic management, road-network efficiency. However, I do know that there must be a cost of fixing it, and that there is a price to be paid for not fixing it. And in my view, whatever is the cost of fixing it cannot be more than a trivial fraction of the cost of not fixing it. Because at the moment we are paying an almost incalculable price for not fixing it. In lost hours, in lost money, and in lost tempers.

Let's face it, the whole thing is a total, complete and utter bloody shambles, and we all sit there like a load of complete bloody wazzocks putting up with it.

It's my belief that if any political party, of any persuasion, came to the electorate with a manifesto that said they were going to sort out the transport system in the UK – (I don't mean an empty promise, but a really credible plan, at no matter what cost) – if a political party did that plausibly, I don't think it would matter if they were also in favour of capital punishment for nuns or of letting rapists out of jails. They could be in favour of dipping dogs in chocolate or force-feeding cats to rats. They could also advocate infanticide or a republic, the abolition of football or being nice to the Germans. No matter what were their other policies, I think they would be elected by a landslide.

Because, whatever the price you had to pay, it would be worth it. Just think. You could go out of your house, find your car in the street outside, climb into it, drive to your destination, arrive in a predictable amount of time, and park when you got there. Blimey!

You could get to a bus stop, and a bus would arrive within a few minutes, you would be able to get on it and would get a seat all the way to your destination. Wow! You could go to a railway station, buy a ticket on the day for the same price that everyone else taking the same journey had paid, and get a seat on the train. The train leaves on time, and you get to your destination when the timetable says you will. Having had a cup of tea en route. What can you say about that?

And not only would we be a happier nation, full of people who were not rushed, stressed, overtired and fed up. We'd also be a lot better off. I don't care what it would cost in infrastructure to achieve what I've just described. The pay back in wellbeing alone would repay the cost in weeks. If you add any calculation of the extra productivity arising from being able to make use of all those utterly futile and wasted hours sitting staring into space and listening to Terry Wogan or whoever is his modern-day equivalent on the radio, we'd be way ahead. Financially and in every other sense too.

Now since this is obvious to me, why isn't it obvious to those who purport to represent us? Why do we put up with being represented and led by lamebrains with no vision, no ideas, and no perception of what the rest of us really want? Instead of the leaflets shoved through your door around election time talking about global warming, or asylum seekers, or litter bins or whatever else it is they talk about, let's talk about something which affects each and every one of us, every day, right here and now.

If these know-nothings talk about transport at all, they talk about carbon emissions or green routes or bus lanes or pedestrian crossings. Trivial tinselling around the edges of the actual problem. Let's have some real leadership by some numerate people. Some people who think about our daily lives, realise the ridiculous misery being caused to every one of us by the dreadful mess that has been made of our transport infrastructure, and do something about it.

Is there any chance of that, do you think? Any chance that we could be led by lions rather than by donkeys? No of course not. I didn't think so. So I remain Grumpy. A Grumpy Old Man. God damn it!

13 Frog crossing

Part of the problem, of course, is that it all creeps up on us.

It's not as if one day life is sensible and straightforward and there are no silly rules or preposterous absurdities, and the next day everything has gone insane.

What happens is that the 'stuff' that gets on the nerve endings of the average Grumpy is added to bit by bit, hour by hour, day by day. It's incremental. It's cumulative.

A good example is the way things look. By which I mean the way things look in the area around you – in the place where you live.

It's not as though one day there was a field with a stream going through it and a hay-wain being towed along by a carthorse, and the next day it was a nightmare of tarmac, traffic islands, road signs, red paint, white paint, yellow paint, stripes, beacons, cat's eyes, railings and speed cameras. All that has happened, but it's all happened one item at a time, so that most people hardly noticed it.

One day someone decided that driving down the middle

of the river was a bit dangerous so they put a track alongside. Next day a few carts had trouble getting by one another and so they widened it in a few places so they could pass. Next day it rained and so they decided to put down some grit to fill in some puddles. The day after that two carts collided at the crossroads and they agreed a speed limit. Day after that someone put up a sign saying what the speed limit was. And so it went on.

It's always fascinating and instructive to look at an old photograph of a busy street or junction that you know well, because the dirt track going between the rows of bakers and haberdashers is now Gateshead High Street. And the shop that was a blacksmith is now a building society and what was an unmarked crossroads is now Clapham Junction. But it all happened one increment at a time, and so most people didn't notice it.

I say 'most people' because another of the many afflictions that are the daily burden of the Grumpy Old Man and the Grumpy Old Woman is that we *do* notice it. We notice it constantly. Even though it is one thing at a time, sometimes days or even weeks apart, we tend to notice the next thing which de-humanises and makes our environment that bit more alienating and offensive. And we comment on it. Regularly.

Oh yes we do.

If you are one of us, as so often, none of this needs to be explained to you. You'll know exactly what I am talking about. If you are a Grumpy and driving into London, the very first time you see a huge Big Brother style notice which proclaims 'Congestion Charge Area – 3 miles', you sigh or swear or exhale one of the heavy sighs you are well known for, to acknowledge yet another infringement of our right to do as we please. Yet another blot on the landscape. Yet another way of ripping us off. Yet another load of old bollocks to add to the rest of the old bollocks that shitheads of one hue or another like to pile upon our heads.

If on the other hand, you are not one of us, you'll probably wonder what the fuss is about.

But if you are in this second happy category and don't know what we are talking about, do me a favour and try a little exercise. It may not do much for you personally, but it will help you to understand the plight of the Grumpy. And we need a lot of understanding.

Do this. Next time you go to your local high street for a spot of shopping, or shoplifting, or whatever it is you do in your local high street, just stop for a moment. I don't mean stop in the middle of the pavement, because that's another thing that irritates Grumpies – people who stand and have their conversation in the middle of the thoroughfare, apparently oblivious to the fact that everyone trying to pass by is having to make a detour.

No, choose a spot where you are out of harm's way, and stand and take a look. Just look, as if with fresh eyes, at the locality you think you know so well, and take a moment to analyse what you are seeing. Take an objective squinley at what the planners, and the councillors, and the highways authority, and the police, and the local authorities collectively have done to the place we all live in.

My guess is that, unless you live in one of those places Prince Charles designed, or approves of, or whatever; unless you live in Highgrove or Poundbury or somewhere like that, the chances are that you are looking at an urban or a suburban nightmare.

First of all take the road signs, and itemize them. '30', cyclists dismount, parking restricted, bridges with height restrictions, width restrictions and weight restrictions. There are signs indicating no left turn, no right turn, no entry, road narrows, give way to traffic coming towards you, or away from you, old people crossing, young children crossing, ducks crossing, deer crossing, or frogs crossing.

Then there will be a whole miscellany of bus lanes, cycle lanes, traffic islands, barriers, Belisha beacons, parking meters, and obelisks to stop cars from trespassing over the edge of the pavement. There are arrows pointing you towards the A3, to 'the south-west', or to Morden, Merton, Malden, Mingdon, or whatever equivalents are local to you.

And then there is the painting on the road. There are the single yellow lines telling you not to park, the double yellow lines telling you not to even think about parking, and accompanying both in case they are not quite in your face enough are the little flashes of double yellow lines on the edge of the pavement. There are red lines for a red route, white lines in the middle of the road, white painted triangles in the middle of the road indicating an upcoming obstacle, and more white chevrons outlining the parts of the road you aren't supposed to drive on.

It won't be enough that someone has written '30' on the upright signs four or five times, now the number '30' will be painted on the road and encircled with another white line to add highlight. There will be a zebra crossing, and on either side of the zebra crossing someone will have painted more white lines in a zig-zag to mark out the approach and the getaway.

There will be stencil outlines of cyclists, and others of mothers with children, and just at the point where it is entirely self-evident that such a lane ends, someone will have stenciled the word 'ENDS'. There will be white lines in boxes indicating where you may park, and more chevrons outside of them to indicate that you may not park. Huge lines will delineate the bus lane, and huge symbols will indicate what vehicles are allowed in them, or are forbidden to be in them. And now and then there will be some experimental design – the roadside version of the Rorschach Inkblot Test – put there to find out what, if anything, we think it means. That's assuming that it could possibly mean anything that hasn't already been indicated one way or another within the visual cacophony of stripes, dots, numbers and chevrons, and that's not even to talk about the sleeping policemen.

So stand back and look at it. Just stand and stare and gape in wonderment. I guarantee that no reasonable person could reach any conclusion other than that the whole place is just a total and utter visual nightmare. An assault on the sensitivities which makes you want to reach for the Kalashnikov just from glancing at it.

Most of these places look to me as though someone has got hold of the kids at the local crèche, given them a load of paint, forced them to drink a bottle of vodka, and told them to have fun.

And by the way, just a little reminder in case you forgot. All of this vandalism and blight on our landscape is perpetrated by people who are paid by you, out of your taxes or rates or whatever, theoretically to make our lives easier. The 'public servants' that we have discussed elsewhere. All stuff done in your name and on your dime. And just look at it. It's the horror show of modern living, and it makes us grumpy. Grumpy Old Men and Grumpy Old Women.

So if by now you are as pissed off by this as are most

Grumpies on a daily basis, and if you've got some time on your hands, it's instructive to consider how many of these signs are actually necessary. What proportion of the signs and arrows and notices and obelisks and warnings and flashing lights, which clutter up your purview on a daily basis, are simply there because they have been invented by people with nothing to do except to dream up answers to problems which don't exist, and to find new ways to spend public money?

Enter 'road traffic symbols' into Google and you'll quickly come to what I reckon by a swift count are 150 different road signs, and that doesn't include variations for turning left versus turning right, or for a 40-mile limit as opposed to a 30. How many of these 150 are surplus to requirements?

What, for example, is the purpose of the warning sign which says on it the single word 'GATE'? What could be the point of that? You're going to be driving along the road, and you are going to come across a gate. Is the sign there designed to tell you what we call it in English? Is it there just in case you are having a temporary senior moment and can't remember what that wooden thing on a hinge with five bars and a diagonal across it is called? What is the fucking point? It's a gate. Get over it!

There is one sign of a galloping horse, which indicates that we should beware of unaccompanied horses, and another of a horse carrying a rider, which indicates that you should watch out for horses with riders on them. What could possibly be the difference?

On the other hand there is one sign which shows a silhouette of a tank, the meaning of which is 'beware of military vehicles', but so far as I can see there is no sub-division of this sign to indicate an armoured personnel carrier or an intercontinental ballistic missile which you might easily come across as you drive across Salisbury Plain.

Believe it or not there is a road sign saying 'no smoking', and another one saying 'try your brakes', and so I am sure we should be grateful that there is no sign of any sign suggesting that you should try your cigarette lighter. Yet.

What are you supposed to do when you are approaching a sign which warns of low-flying aircraft? Duck? What are you supposed to do when you see a sign indicating 'weak bridge' – go on a diet? What are you supposed to do when you see a sign which says 'heavy plant crossing' – water it? Has anyone ever seen a frog crossing a road? And what are you supposed to do if you do? There is one sign indicating that we should beware of cattle and another suggesting that we should beware of sheep. What is the difference? Could it be that, having been warned of sheep, we are allowed to plough into the cattle? And vice versa? And why, then, is there no sign suggesting that we should beware of pigs or goats – either or both of which are every bit as likely to wander across the road where I spend a lot of my time.

Does anyone ever wonder what we did before we had all this guff shoved in our collective faces every minute of every day? Presumably we must have survived somehow.

But anyway, the point is that our streets – the places we live in – have become ugly. Cluttered, crowded, a blur of hideous and unnecessary instructions, warnings, information, and general impertinence designed to make our lives more regimented and more complicated. It's alienating and it's repugnant and it makes us care less about our environment, which leads to more graffiti of the unofficial kind and all that follows from that.

Grumpies hate all this stuff. We'd like to rip it all out of the ground, stick it on a bloody great big bonfire, place the bureaucrats and busybodies who dreamed it all up on top, and light a match. And in the unlikely event that anyone ever puts us in charge, we will.

14 A–Z

Do you think that the people who publish the *A–Z* are taking the piss?

I mean it. Do you think they can be serious, or are they just having a little bit of fun at our expense? If the latter, I could almost forgive them. I'd find that so much more endearing than the idea that they want to be taken seriously. However, I fear that maybe they aren't trying to have a laugh, and that they believe there is someone, somewhere, at some time, who isn't infuriated by their sodding maps.

As I tip out of the wrong end of what are supposed to be the core years of Grumpiness (35–54) it's my proud boast that more or less the only thing about me that is still working reasonably well is my eyesight. Dunno why, and maybe it's my body's idea of compensating for all the other manifold ways in which it has let me down in recent years, but unaccountably my eyesight still isn't too bad.

At least, that's what I think until I want to look up something in the *A–Z*.

Now it ought to be said that in recent years I have deliberately been buying jumbo versions of the *A–Z* in the hope that I can make head or tail of it. My current one says BIG LONDON A–Z on the cover in blue and red letters so huge that they could be read from a passing 747. But for these purposes, and to illustrate my point, I have dug out an old copy in the standard format.

Let's turn first of all to the index. The street names are written in five vertical columns, and I'm going to ask the publisher of this book if we can reproduce a few words in the same size as this stuff is printed, just to make the point. I think it's probably in what printers call 6 point and it looks like this.

St George's Sq. SW1 - 5H **77** (6C **154**)
St George's Ter. NW1 - 7D **44**
St George St. W1 - 7F **61** (1K **147**)
St George's Wlk. Croy - 3C **134**
St George's Way. SE15 - 6E **78**
St Gerards Clo. SW4 - 5G **93**

Can you read that?

Sorry – I meant – Can you read that? Of course you can't, and my bet is that if you can it's because you are sitting in an armchair or propped up in bed, perfectly stationary, with a good strong light behind you. Either that or you are bloody Superman, in which case you should be out righting wrongs.

So now try to imagine or remind yourself what it's like attempting to read the same thing when you are in your car, it's late at night, the map-reading light in your vehicle is about as much use as the proverbial candle in the wind, the reflection of flashing red lights and amber lights and fluorescent lights is bouncing off the roof and spilling onto the page, and you are rocking about because inter-continental juggernauts are hurtling past with the grace, speed and abandon of

Members of European Parliament on their way to a free lunch.

Do you have any chance now? No, I thought not. So, as even an idiot could work out that these are the most likely circumstances in which most of us are going to be consulting the index of the A–Z, what do you think they are playing at?

I don't suppose that anyone sensible enough to be reading this book could also be so unhelpful or uncharitable as to be thinking 'well, you should have thought of that before you started out, and looked up the route before you left home.' And if you are so unhelpful and uncharitable as to be thinking that, then most likely you are a person of the female persuasion.

Grumpy Old Men very seldom look at the map before we set out for a journey. We know the way. Or we more or less know the way, and we feel certain that once we get in the area it'll all become clear to us. The trouble is that once we do get into the area we find it's all changed since we were last here as a teenager, and we're hopelessly and utterly lost. And since there can be no question of a Grumpy Old Man ever asking directions, it is only now that we will reluctantly resort to consulting the A–Z. But it's dark, and it's cold, and it's windy, and already we're as irritated as hell, and that's before we start to try to decipher the index.

The next thing that is irritating about the index of the A–Z is that items aren't listed in the correct order. Does it seem that way to you? To take a random example; the index goes from Heather Close, to Heatherdale Close, and then to Heather Drive. How can that be right? Aren't you supposed to finish all the names beginning with 'Heather' before you go on to 'Heatherdale'? The upshot of all this and related irritations is that, three times out of five, I cannot find the place I want to go to when I consult the index. Is that just me?

But for the sake of pressing on, let's imagine that you have found, can read, and can turn to the place you want to locate. Is anyone able to tell me why it is always tucked right down into the fold between the pages? How can that be? The law of averages tells you that this is going to happen a small proportion of the time, but I find that it happens every time. Or, if not every time, at least every second time. How can it be that 50 per cent of the places you want to look up are on the cusp? How heinous an act must I have committed in a former life to make that so in this one?

Actually, to be fair, the copy I am consulting for the purposes of this exercise is bound together with a ring-binder and so some aspects of this exasperating phenomenon are alleviated. Still, however, even a cursory examination of this volume shows many examples of the names of roads which are already printed in letters so small that you'd need an electron microscope to read them, cut in half with the top of the letters written on page 145 and the bottom of the letters written on page 144. Or vice versa.

And that's always the place I want to go.

No matter how short a distance I need to cover, my journey always seems to start in the top right-hand corner of a right-hand page, to spill over to the bottom left-hand corner of another one five pages further on, and then to bend down again to resume its course on the page following the one I started with. So basically I am never really on the correct page. Ever.

Add to that the fact that, three times out of five, the red dot containing the grid reference letter or number is printed over the name of the road I was looking for, and it's all added up to a fairly unhappy experience. Which you'd think would persuade people who are Grumpy even before they start out, to prepare better or maybe to acquire for themselves one of those ingenious little gadgets which are supposed to do your navigation for you ... but that's another story.

15 Women drivers

Wherever I go I am, as you might imagine, overjoyed to be introduced as 'that Grumpy old bastard who writes those books and TV series'. It always makes my day. And when that happens, all too often I am treated to someone's view about whether the men are funnier than the women, or the other way around. I am sure you can probably guess just how much fun that is for me.

It seems that some people think the men are funnier, others think the women are funnier, and oddly enough the breakdown of opinion isn't, as you might expect, strictly along the lines of gender. Plenty of women seem to think that the Grumpy Old Men are funnier, and vice versa.

When asked what the difference between their humour is I, of course, demur. However, one observation I sometimes make is that Grumpy Old Women seem to be only too happy to indulge in a very good line of everything that is irritating about Grumpy Old Men, whereas Grumpy Old Men never do the reverse.

No we don't. Grumpy Old Men never talk about what makes

them grumpy about women because, whatever else Grumpy Old Men could justly be accused of, for the most part we are not stupid. No, we're not stupid, and we know enough to know that this is a moment to be careful. Very, very careful.

However, when it comes to the subject of Grumpy Old Driving, it doesn't seem to me that there is any way of escaping the fact that women drive differently from men. I am not going to say that women drive less well. I am not going to say that they drive better. All I am saying is that the way that men and women drive is different.

So I wonder what is the best way to sum up the difference? It's not easy to do so while remaining within the bounds of what is acceptable but, if pressed for a simple summary, I think you would have to say that the difference between men and women is that women drive by the rules.

What that means at its most basic is that, for example, women keep their car on their side of the road, making sure that they don't cross the line painted down the middle. This is my side of the road, and that's your side. You don't come across on my side, and I won't go across on your side.

That's a very good plan, and for the most part it works well. When it doesn't work quite so well, though, is when the person approaching you from the other direction might be veering just a little bit over your side of the road. Or it may be that a motorcyclist coming the other way is overtaking a car and seems to be on your side of the road for longer than is comfortable.

Whereas the average male driver will see this coming and might perhaps nudge his car just a little over to the left to give room for the bloke approaching from the other way just in case, the average woman driver doesn't do that. She is on her

side of the road. She is following the rules. That white line marks the middle. This is her bit, and that's your bit. If you are on her bit, you shouldn't be, and so if there is an accident that's your lookout.

The fact that the potential consequences of 'your lookout' are likely to be just as serious for her as they are for the oncoming car or motorcycle seems to be secondary to following the rules. She is obeying the Highway Code, and that's that. She's on her side, and you should be keeping on yours.

This is also the reason why a lot of women drivers tend to stop if there is a white line at the entrance to a roundabout. The fact that you can see from half a mile away that there is no traffic on the roundabout is neither here nor there. It's a white line. You are supposed to stop at white lines. The impatient bastard behind blasting his horn and slapping his forehead with the palm of his hand can go and screw himself. I am following the rules.

I believe that this is also why I've heard a lot of women say that they prefer not to drive in central London, or in Paris or Rome for that matter. It's because a lot of big cities throw everyone into a bloody big space, and let you sort yourselves out when you get there. Enormous roundabouts with lots of exits and no clear lanes guiding you between one and the next. The rules aren't clear, and so everything they have learned goes to hell.

Does any of this ring a bell? Women drive because they have learned to do so, and men drive on instinct. No doubt men are on the whole more reckless. No doubt men on the whole cause more accidents. But how many of us – men or women – could honestly say that they prefer to be driven by a woman than by a man?

Well I said we were getting into dangerous territory.

I know that it's unfair to generalise. The risk of being unfair doesn't usually worry a Grumpy too much, but over the years we have tended to develop quite sharp antennae for when we're sailing close, and – like *My Favourite Martian* – my antennae are twitching furiously.

In order, therefore, to avoid generalising any further I'm going to move swiftly from the general to the particular, and to talk about women drivers as exemplified by my wife. She is a good sport and, anyway, already has plans for how to spend the royalties from this book.

My wife came a little bit later in life to driving than did most people, and I used to like it before she could drive because in those days she was very helpful to me as a passenger. The reason for this is because her sense of direction was so awful that it could quite frequently prove to be useful.

So bad was it in fact that, if I was approaching a road junction and was in doubt as to which way to turn, I would sometimes ask her what she thought. She would, with an almost uncanny degree of reliability, get the answer 180 degrees wrong. So that if she said 'I would turn left' I would turn right, and if she said 'I would turn right' I would turn left, and that was almost always the right decision. See what I mean? Extremely useful.

Once she learned to drive, however, my wife was of course obliged to develop at least a rudimentary sense of direction, otherwise she would never have been able to get home. The result, I regret to say, is that the reliability I was once able to place on her being almost always wrong has been eroded and, on the very rare occasions that I ask her opinion on which way we should go, she is about as likely to be right as she is to be wrong – i.e. she is no use at all in this respect.

Having said that we were moving from the general to the specific, I cannot avoid just throwing in the observation that my wife is by no means alone in this respect. And if you don't believe me, you can try this one for yourself. Next time you are in a place where there is a mix of men and women, ask them all at the same time to point north. I rest my case.

My wife's sense of direction is still sufficiently bad that she knows only one way back from the supermarket, and if there is a road closure on that route she is perfectly likely to do a detour around a complete circuit of the M25 before she arrives home. She would freely admit that road signs like 'ring road west' or 'ring road east' might as well be written in Swahili for all the use they are to her. Likewise, she admits that three times out of five she forgets where she has left the car in the multi-storey car park.

On top of all that, my wife also hates driving at night – claiming that the glare from oncoming headlights is blinding – so that quite often she keeps her own headlights on full beam. Last time she did this a bloke in front of her at the traffic lights nipped out to tell her courteously that it might be a good idea to drive with dipped headlights in the city centre. He also nipped out again at the next set of lights to show her politely which switch she needed to push in order to dip the headlights.

But to be quite fair to her, my wife is of course an excellent driver, and if this were not the case I certainly wouldn't be writing about it here. I know she is an excellent driver because she's been driving for about 20 years in all sorts of circumstances and has never yet had a mishap. Though not of a superstitious disposition myself, I am aware of the risk of seeming to tempt fate, so as I write this I am crossing my fingers and touching wood and all that old bollocks, and hoping that it is all old bollocks.

I say that her incident-free record is my evidence that she is an excellent driver because, of course, I have no other evidence available to me. This is because my wife will not drive the car while I am in it.

To be fair, this is not an absolutely hard and fast rule. On one or two occasions I have had a minor surgical operation and have had to be ferried back from the hospital while still partially under the influence of the anaesthetic. In these limited circumstances – i.e. me being semi-conscious – she will agree to take the wheel while I am in the passenger seat. Also, in other very rare circumstances, such as for example if she were to pass me in the street no more than 50 yards from home, she might give me a lift. However, there are very few other occasions when this can happen.

The reason is, of course, that my wife is a very good driver, but that I make her into a very bad driver. It's all my fault, because I make her nervous. Left to herself she is calm, in control, on top of the situation, perfectly able. With me sitting next to her in the passenger seat, she drives like Helen Keller on her first driving lesson. In a Chieftain tank. In the fog. Except more dangerous.

Ordinarily, when driving alone or with one of her girlfriends in the car, I am assured that my wife will arrive at a road junction, wait for a suitable gap, and then proceed away in a smooth and flowing manner. When I am sitting beside her, on the other hand, she is quite likely to stall the engine, thereby causing the person behind her to blast on their horn, which obviously has the effect of calming her down and thus enabling her to re-start the engine and pull away smoothly.

Alternatively, she might kangaroo away from a junction, or turn on the windscreen wipers when she intends to turn on the indicator. Likely as not she'll try to pull away without releasing the handbrake, whereupon I cannot stop myself from releasing it for her, which of course only makes matters worse.

She claims that when she is driving alone she doesn't think about when to change the gears – she just changes them. When I am with her, she seems to feel the need to think about it and so changes too early, or too late, and often not at all. It's not easy to know what to say when you are bombing down a dual carriageway doing 60 in third gear.

Usually in these circumstances, because I know my presence makes her tense, I'll just do everything possible to seem as casual as I can. Totally relaxed. I'll look out of the side window, whistle softly, sit back in my seat as though considering going off for a short nap. However, none of this works, and in any and all circumstances where my wife is driving and I am in the car, she behaves as though she is being held hostage by Darth Vader and forced to drive to the Death Star.

If, after two or three incidents of stalling, or crunches of the gearbox, or mounting the kerb as the pensioners are queuing outside the post office, I make the mistake of enquiring whether there is anything wrong, the answer is vehement and unambiguous.

'It's you!'

'Me? Why? What am I doing?'

'You're sitting there!'

'Yes, I know that. I am sitting here. As a passenger in the car, there's not a lot else I can do.'

'But you are sitting there being critical.'

'What?'

'You are. I can just tell that you are watching everything I do and being critical.'

And of course there is simply nothing I can say to that. How does one sit still and try to appear not to be critical? The more you try, the worse it gets. I once even tried appearing to read a newspaper while being driven along by my wife, but that didn't work because apparently I was rustling the pages in a critical way – or something.

So usually we go out in my car, and when we go out in her car I'll drive. And I have to try to remember to drive her car from time to time because quite often when I do there will be a warning light on the dashboard – indicating that something or other needs attention.

'How long has that been coming on?' I might enquire.

'I don't know.'

'Well what do you think? A day, a week, a month?'

'I don't know, I never look down there,' which is a bit of a worry because the warning lights are next to the speedometer.

'It might be as well to tell me when you see a warning light go on,' I'll gently suggest, 'because it could be important. That's why they call them warning lights.'

On the odd occasions when I drive her car I might also take the opportunity to check the oil (she doesn't know how to open the bonnet), reset the clock to British Summer Time (she doesn't know how to adjust the clock), refill the windscreen washer (turns out it's been empty since Whit), and reset the radio away from the grunge station it has inadvertently been set to. And if I look in the boot I might ask why she seems to have been carrying around a big suitcase full of clothes for several months – and the answer will be that she has been meaning to drop it off at the charity shop, but hasn't got around to it.

Yes, women drive very differently from men. I'm not saying worse. I am not saying better. Just differently. Is that safe to say?

16 Flats

Has anyone, ever, in the history of the world driven their car into one of those 'tyre, exhaust, battery' places and not been told they need a new tyre? Or, indeed, that you need two new tyres? Has that ever happened to you? It's never happened to me.

Obviously there are no circumstances in which you would go into one of these places unless you had an immediate problem. We're not masochists for heaven's sake. But the idea that you'd drive in, be greeted by an open and winning smile, a quick 'that's no problem, sir, we'll have that mended in five minutes' and be charged the cost of a puncture repair, is so far from reality that it reads like a fairy story.

It's not as though you are in an especially good mood even when you get there. Your visit is usually going to be the culmination of what has already been an ordeal lasting several hours, which started at 7am when you came out of your house, dressed in your business clothes, late for an appointment, and found the tyre to be flat.

There is never any obvious reason for it. Never. You find yourself wondering momentarily whether the local brats have let your tyre down overnight. You walk around the others and give them a kick. The mystery is never susceptible to an immediate solution.

Obviously it's still dark, the weather is cold and wet, and you had been intending for some months to clear out the garage to make enough space to accommodate the car, but you never got around to it. Because that's how life is.

About now you remember that you have also been intending to locate the spare wheel and everything you would need to change a tyre, before circumstances like these obliged you to do so in a hurry. You didn't. So now you have to go back indoors, put on your old clothes, and start by opening the boot and removing everything that has accumulated there since you bought the car – that'll be the kids' Wellingtons, a half-empty bottle of water, a kite, an umbrella, a ragged map-book, some old newspapers, the de-icing spray, etc, etc.

Next you have to try to get your fingers under the edge of a piece of carpet, and below that you come to a large and unwieldy piece of hardboard. You can't find a corner, or any other way to lift it up, and eventually begin to wonder if it comes up at all. Maybe the spare wheel in this car is kept somewhere else. Underneath? You go and find a piece of old carpet from the garage so you can lie on your back and take a look. Where is that torch? Finally you give that up and return to the boot with renewed determination. At last you might get a fingertip under a corner and lift, grazing the skin off your knuckles and emitting a loud curse as you do so. Any of this sound familiar?

If you are lucky, you will eventually find a spare wheel way down in the bowels of the car, and more often than not it'll be one of those lightweight 'get you home' efforts, which looks like someone has mistakenly replaced your wheel with a spare taken off a perambulator.

So now you need to find the jack which is not in with the spare wheel where you'd expect it to be, but has been carefully located in a secret cupboard somewhere else. Occasionally about now you might stumble across a first-aid kit and think 'that's handy'. If and when you do eventually find the jack, it is encased in a polystyrene moulding with no clue or indication as to which way up it's supposed to go. It looks like a medieval instrument of torture and, in the event of even the most trivial mishandling, has the same potential for giving pain.

Is there anyone, do you think, anywhere on the planet who has ever had to do one of these jobs, and just got it right first time? Anyone anywhere who knows which way this goes into that? Who can immediately locate the bracket or hole or clip or whatever it is underneath the car that the thing is supposed to slot into? Is there anyone who doesn't start to jack up the car and realise that the whole thing is wonky and liable to imminent collapse with unspeakable consequences? I guess there is such a person, but if there is I certainly haven't met him. And I do say 'him' advisedly, because my guess is that if such a person exists it's fairly certain to be a 'him'. Men are bad enough at this sort of thing but women are, by and large and with very few exceptions, hopeless.

Can anyone answer me this? How does an ordinary person loosen wheel nuts? You've watched them being tightened in the garage by a bloke putting his 20 stone of weight on them, or by one of those awesome mechanical drill-like machines out of *Mad Max Beyond the Thunderdome*. Now you have to loosen them in your drive, or at the side of the motorway.

Place the spanner over the nut. Push down. It doesn't move. Push harder. Not a sign of movement. Put all your weight on it. The spanner comes loose from the nut suddenly and you scrape your hand on the road, or the wheel, or the wheel arch and it starts to bleed copiously. Blood and grease mixed together and bound up with an oily rag is always fun – no doubt good for getting the old autoimmune system going.

Next you attempt to angle the spanner so that you can stand on it and use all your weight to try to prize it loose. Most likely the spanner won't fit firmly enough over the nut for it to be able to bear your weight. You deduce that the spanner needs to be supported at the handle end, and go to try to find something of the same height off the road as the nut, to rest it on. Maybe an old oil can? Maybe the spare wheel laid on its side? No, nothing is quite the right height.

One way or another you eventually find a way to keep the spanner on the nut while you stand on it and gently bounce up and down trying to ease it loose. If eventually you do, it slackens suddenly and you plummet towards the earth and a likely sprained ankle.

A bit of sweat and bother and the imminent risk of a hernia, and three nuts out of four are loosened. Now the fourth. A problem. The spanner won't go over the nut. Why might that be? Try it this way. Try it that way. But no. It won't fit on this way, it won't fit on that way.

You turn the spanner upside down, look at it back to front, scour the garage for other similar spanners, hit it with a monkey wrench, and still cannot make head nor tail of it.

It is then, and only then, that you discover that one of the nuts is of a different shape and design from the other three. Of course ... because up until now it was all going so well.

You go back into the house to try to find the car manual. What – the hell – is going on? It's not bad enough, apparently, that you have a flat tyre and have to change it at what can never be your leisure or convenient circumstances. No, let's see if we can think of a new obstacle to make life just a little bit more difficult.

Eventually you locate the mock-leather pochette containing the automobile equivalent of *Gray's Anatomy*, which instructs you how to drive the car, and you look in the index. What will it be listed under? F for 'flat tyres'? No. S for 'spare wheel'? No. C for 'changing a ...' No. Will it be under 'I' for 'if someone somewhere doesn't give me a fucking break in the next ten minutes I'll top myself'? No, It's under W for 'wheels'. Dah daa!

Was there something in here about a secret password or handshake? Something about a concealed decoder ring listed in the manual?

So obviously you already know, because you are a smart alec, that the very clever manufacturers of very clever cars have introduced a cunning device to prevent hoodlums from jacking up your vehicle and making off with the wheels. A little metal jacket which is supposed to fit snugly inside the hole in the spanner and then slide neatly over the fourth nut on the wheel. Excellent.

Now you think you've got it. Where is this secret-coded spanner-insert, or whatever it's called? Where could it be? Could it have been in that little package that was in the glove compartment, but which we put in the garage somewhere when we were clearing out the car because we had no idea what it was?

Eventually you locate it, insert the little metal jacket thingy into the spanner, loosen the fourth and final nut, and only then do you discover that you haven't lifted the car high enough on the jack to be able to remove the wheel, and only then do you realise that the car is on a slight camber and that, the more you jack it up, the more the wheels have angled themselves inwards to compensate for the fact that the car thought it was going round a corner.

By now you are at the uppermost limit of the jack and still can't get the wheel off. So after looking at it this way, and looking at it that way, and walking around it, and making a cup of tea and kicking the car a couple of times, eventually you accept that there is no alternative but to re-tighten the nuts, lower the car, move it a few yards or place a plank of wood under the jack, and start again.

In slightly more time than it took to complete the D-Day landings, you eventually get the wheel off. Now comes the task of putting the spare one on. It's heavy. It's very, very heavy and you have to bend over like a bloody double-jointed ballerina to be able to lift it onto the nuts. And can you position the replacement wheel so that the holes align smoothly over the bolts on the axle, and fit smoothly on? Can you support the weight of the spare wheel while trying to crane your head to one side to get them lined up accurately? I'm going to stop now because I'm getting annoyed just writing it.

The bloody hours and hours of sodding about – on the sides of roads, or at the house, or at someone else's house, or outside a hotel, or wherever – that most of us have wasted on shit like this, makes you want to weep like a newborn baby. It makes you want to curl up into a foetal position, stick your greasy thumb in your mouth, and hold on tight to that little square of blue blanket that was taken away from you all too soon at the age of 12.

Then, and this is where we came in, whenever you have a puncture, change the wheel, and put the injured tyre in the boot, there comes the unavoidable joy of a visit to the tyre and exhaust centre. Even as you drive into these places your heart is sinking. You feel as though you could pre-script what is about to happen with an uncanny degree of accuracy. It's never any different.

First of all you park outside the workshop and stand there like a lemon for as long as it takes for one of them to deign to notice you. Like waiters in an expensive French restaurant, they have developed a very clever knack of avoiding your eye until they are good and ready. At this stage you are still very keen not to piss them off because you are in their territory, you are miles out of your depth, and you're still nurturing a forlorn hope that what you know will happen next, won't happen next.

The blokes who work in these places are another set who all came off the same production line. I won't go into detail because I don't want to seem more of a supercilious prat than is inevitable – but maybe we should just say that they're not much like the singing and dancing troop of men dressed in blue overalls who proclaim in song that *'you can't get better than a Kwik-Fit fitter'* or whatever the hell it is. No, if that group of people works anywhere in the tyre and exhaust empire, it's certainly not in any of their garages which I have had the pleasure of visiting.

If and when you ever get their attention, you'll say something like 'I had a puncture' and lead them towards the boot. Someone who looks like the boss will come over and lift the wheel up and out with the same ease as you would lift your pencil-case, and roll it across a yellow painted line beyond which you are not allowed to tread, and into the inner sanctum.

Five minutes will pass. Actually of course they know, and you know, exactly what is coming next, and it doesn't take five minutes for anyone to work it out. However, someone on their side of the business has decreed that, if they don't take five minutes to tell you what the problem is, it'll look as though they haven't examined your tyre properly. So you have to wait for five minutes.

And guess what. You need a new tyre. I reckon that in 38 years of driving, some version of the above has probably happened to me about 20 times, and I can honestly say that I have never had an experience where the bloke has said 'oh yes, it's just got a nail in it. We can patch that up in no time.' No. Usually it's not the puncture, but the 'wall of the tyre' has somehow been damaged beyond recall. Someone must have driven on the flat. Come and look. Oh yes, very dangerous. It might last you 50 miles but then it could go very suddenly ...

Even though you studied hard at school, maybe went on to further education, maybe you have run a business, maybe employed loads of people, none of this is of any use to you. You are entirely in his hands. You may be able to perform a surgical operation, produce a set of certified accounts or split the atom, but you do not have the knowledge or experience or the confidence to say 'you are talking out of your arse my friend,' because he may be telling a lie, and he may be telling the truth. You just have no way of knowing.

All that *Beowulf*, or Latin, or Algebra, or History or *Paradise Lost* has given you absolutely no equipment or qualification to know whether this nasty, shifty-looking little shit is lying to you. No amount of iambic pentameters can save you now.

So you hear yourself saying 'have you got one?' and then he goes to his computer and he has never got one. I don't think

that in all my lifetime of experience of all this stuff he's ever had one. But, wait for it … he's always got 'the equivalent'.

Yes, the Michelin X47A9 is more or less the same as the Pirelli 192XP1 if you don't want to corner too hard, or something. How much? £97. Excellent – a week's wages for many people gone down the drain because of a tack in the road. The joy.

And that's not to mention the exhaust …!

17 If you were a car ...

If you were a car, what kind of car would you be?

Have you ever been asked that question? It's a variation, I think, on those standard psychology questions such as 'if you were a kind of animal, what kind of animal would you be?' Designed by some pointy-head somewhere to find out something about you that you'd probably rather the world didn't know.

If you say 'a lion' you are an arrogant sod. If you say 'a fox' you are a devious bastard. If you say 'a panda' you are gay. You know the sort of thing.

Anyway, reluctant as I am to admit it, I think that the kind of car you drive frequently does give us the opportunity for a sneaky little peek into your personality. I think I've recorded before that my old friend Alan Lewens, producer of the first two series of *Grumpy Old Men*, believes that all BMW drivers have a recordably lower IQ than the average. I'm not entirely sure where this delightful prejudice came from – perhaps from some regrettable personal experience – but nonetheless he harbours it with great and entertaining conviction.

Beyond that, however, I think that one could advance a very respectable theory that your choice of car tells us something about you.

The Volvo is an obvious example. What do we think about the average driver of the Volvo Estate? Solid. Cautious. Safety-conscious. Quite well-to-do. Probably with a family. Maybe either towing a caravan or with a secret hankering to do so. Green wellies.

See what I mean? It's not rocket science. Easy peasy.

I think something similar goes for cars like Jaguars. If you drive a Jaguar you are probably a bit of a show-off. The manager of a first division football team, something like that. Saabs – perhaps you are just a tiny bit unconventional. Certainly the Toyota Prius – save the planet and more money than sense. I won't go through the characteristics because you know them as well as I do.

However, what is much more entertaining, I think, is to reflect on the cases where the signals about us we *think* are being sent out by our cars are so very different from the signals about us which are *actually* being sent out by our cars.

The most obvious example that we are all familiar with is the balding middle-aged saddo in the Porsche. It's the car he desperately wanted but couldn't afford when he was 19. Now he's 50 and he can afford it, and he isn't going to be put off by the fact that his paunch all but prevents him from getting in it. Lid down, straggly hair carefully arranged under a baseball cap, shades, bombing down the outside lane thinking he's as cool as iced tea.

These days there is even a subtle twist on this phenomenon because the middle-aged bloke driving the Porsche kinda

knows, on some level, that he is indeed cutting a rather pathetic figure rather than the one he hankers after. So he adopts a facial expression which says 'I know but I don't care.' A kind of 'you might think I'm a prat but I'm going to enjoy it anyway.' However, unfortunately there is no getting away from the fact that his enjoyment is all but entirely marred by the knowledge that people aren't so much thinking 'isn't he cool', but more like 'what a tool'.

Less obvious, though, are some of the variations, and I think it might be instructive, as well as a springboard for a lively debate in your household, to consider the contrasts between the impression perceived by the owner, and the impression actually received by the observer – if you see what I mean. Let's go a bit wild, break with convention, and construct a little table:

Car	Impression hoped for	Impression actually given
Citroën 2 CV	Hippy	Sad throwback
Ford Mustang	Steve McQueen	A bit of a wanker
Aston Martin	James Bond	A bit of a wanker
Bentley	Suave, sophisticated	Wanker
Maserati	Playboy	Wanker
Ferrari	David Beckham	Total wanker

All right all right, we've all noticed that there is starting to emerge a fairly dull consistency in the right-hand column, but I ask you?

18 Two wheels good

My way of trying to hang on to even a remote semblance of sanity in all this bloody mayhem is to ride a motorcycle.

I've been riding motorbikes on and off since I was 16, and when I reached the age of 40 I ceremonially gave away what I thought would be my last one – a blue Honda Super-Dream. I was living just outside Manchester at the time and, although the traffic in and out of work at Granada TV in Quay Street was terrible and getting worse, I decided that it was just about bearable to do my commute in a car. Anyway, I felt that at 40 I was far too old to be buzzing around the place on two wheels.

However, a year or two after that a new job at the ITV Network Centre meant that I had to move back to London. We chose our location on the basis of what would be convenient for the kids' school, as you do, and so I was living in Kingston, working in Gray's Inn Road, and driving an hour and a half across town in the morning and an hour and a half across town in the evening. Three hours a day, fifteen hours in an average working week, just sitting in my car and trying to prevent my brain from turning to porridge with boredom and frustration. The only upside of this arrangement was that I became addicted to *The Archers*. The downside was that, taking account of the time demanded by work and the commute to and from, I never had time for a life.

Since some of you will no doubt be wondering why I didn't take public transport, the answer is that this would have involved a walk, then a bus, then a train and then the tube again and a walk, or another bus, and all in the rush hour. That would be when the public transport in our area decided to run, which was not all that often. To adopt this alternative would undoubtedly have proven to be a quicker route for me to an early grave even than sitting in the car.

When you do the same car journey every day, day in day out, and are always in the same tearing hurry, it becomes a series of obstacles and challenges which you set yourself. The continuing running commentary in your head which we have described before, now goes something like this: *if I get through these traffic lights, and put my foot down, I can reach the next one before it turns red. On the other hand, if I get stuck behind that clown in the three-wheeler I'll be held up. I need to get into the inside lane round this bend, but then filter quickly over to the other lane sometime before the next pedestrian crossing. A little slalom around these sleeping policemen ..., brake hard as we go past this speed camera ... the police often tuck themselves out of sight in this lay-by. Just made it through the lights. Phew ...'* Etc, etc.

If all goes well and you drive like one of those upper-class nitwits from *The Italian Job* (the original, obviously), maybe you can knock as much as ten minutes off your journey. If not, and you miss the lights, get stuck in the wrong lane because no bugger will let you in, have to wait while 150 school children cross on the crossing, it can add 10 minutes. A difference of 20 minutes a day, in each direction, adds up to 40 minutes of time I could otherwise spend doing something useful, or useless, but anyway use as I want to, rather than struggling through traffic. In the world of the motoring commuter, such things take on an importance out of all proportion to their real significance.

Or it could be worse than that, and this is what eventually happened to me. Worse than that is when you find that you go onto autopilot. You've done this journey so many times that you get in the car and switch off your brain until you reach your destination. It was when I started to find that I had arrived home, or arrived at work, and couldn't remember a single thing about the last hour and a half, that I began to wonder if this was good for me. Or for the other people using the roads. If I had no recollection of that junction, or traffic light, or pedestrian crossing, it seemed unlikely that I could be concentrating hard enough for it to remain safe. Has this happened to you?

Anyway, just like everyone else, I found myself sitting in my car, not moving, as the blokes on motorbikes and scooters ducked and weaved through the traffic. I watched with a mixture of hatred and envy, and I wondered. Would I still feel able, aged 43 and well into my Grumpy years, to go back to riding a motorcycle on a daily basis? Having one as a toy and getting it out of the garage occasionally on a fine day for a ride through the countryside is one thing, but using it for a daily commute through some of the busiest traffic anywhere in the world felt like quite another.

Eventually I decided that my choices were to find out, or to leave London, or to die. It was that simple. If I continued sitting in all this traffic, eventually I would hyperventilate, burst a blood-vessel, or kill or be killed in an altercation with the

driver of one of those bendy buses which is going to keep on coming whether you are in the way or not.

So I borrowed a motorbike from my brother Steve for a few days – he happened to have an old Yamaha sitting in the garage – just to see whether I still had the bottle to do it. I tried it for a few days, round the South Circular across from west London, over the Thames and through Holborn, and I think it's fair to say that I found the experience terrifying. Absolutely bloody terrifying. Weaving in and out between the traffic, being blown about on any short piece of open road, wiping the teaming rain off the visor to try to get some idea of what was going on all around, kamikaze cyclists and pedestrians all but throwing themselves under your wheels, dogs threatening to run into the road, wet manhole covers, the whole works.

However, at the end of a week it remained clear to me that I had a choice between risking death by terror or collision on the motorbike, or death by frustration and boredom which would inevitably follow if I continued sitting in a car.

So I bought myself a Kawasaki 750 and started to use it to commute.

That was about 14 years ago and, looking back on it, I can think of those first few years as a golden age. Obviously the whole thing was a nightmare, and I was constantly at risk from the idiot who suddenly decides to fling open his car door to try to identify the cause of the hold-up ahead, or thinks this brief stop would be a good opportunity to leap out of the car to remove his jacket – and my head at the same time. Obviously bus drivers didn't give a damn if you were on the inside of them when they were turning left. Equally obviously I faced the ever-present danger from the van driver to whom it doesn't occur to stop at a junction. But even given all that, 14 years ago it was all so much better than it is today.

What has been the big change since then? What has been the thing that has made the life of anyone on two wheels so much more flimsy today than it was around 1990? Well, let's get to that in a moment, but start just a wee bit earlier.

The only point, I am sure everyone would agree, of using a motorbike or scooter, is so that you can ride along between or outside the crawling lines of cars. Though I know that some car-drivers find this irritating, I always think I'm doing them a favour because otherwise I would be in my car, and further adding to the delay they are already experiencing. I know that very few car drivers see it this way, but I do.

Also, it seems a fair trade-off – you, the motorist, are sitting in a nice warm armchair, remaining dry, listening to the radio, and will arrive safe, tidy and (probably) late. I on the other hand am sitting bolt upright, probably getting soaked, risking life and limb and will arrive dishevelled but (probably) on time. Choose your poison. Live and let live and all that.

Be that as it may, the motorcyclist is essentially at the mercy of the four-wheeled motorist. Our lives are in their hands and, having had plenty of time and opportunity to make a careful study of it, I have come to the view that there are five possible alternative behaviours by the drivers of cars in relation to motorbikes. Bear with me – these won't take long.

Alternative 1: by and large you will find that ordinary blokes, who once rode a bike themselves but probably now no longer do so, will spot you in their wing mirrors and, if possible, nudge over an inch or two to give you some room to go by. When anyone does that for me, I always give them a wave of thanks as I pass. It makes everyone's day go just a little bit easier. These people fall into the general description of decent human beings.

Alternative 2: people who see you in their mirror, realise that if they moved just a few inches to the right, you could get through, but don't bother to do so. This usually involves blokes rather like those in the last category – but instead of thinking 'I'll let the poor bastard through', they're thinking something like 'if I have to be held up, why shouldn't he get held up?' or something equally ungenerous. Generally these people come under the heading of arseholes.

Alternative 3 consists of the people who see you there, alongside their car on one side or another, but it just doesn't occur to them that they could make everyone's life easier by getting out of the way. They're in their lane. They're following the rules. They're not trying to hold you up, and they're not trying to help you along. You are in their mirror but not on their radar. This category, I am sorry to say, usually involves women. Best to describe these people as airheads.

Alternative 4 is the people who probably know what the rear-view mirror inside their car is for – it's for looking in to make sure that their fringe is straight. On the other hand they really have no idea what the wing mirrors are for. If they're adjusted correctly at all, they're never glanced into. These people don't see you, and don't care that they haven't seen you. You may as well not exist. My shorthand for these people is fuckwits.

Finally, and least attractive of all, alternative 5 consists of the people who see you coming up behind in their mirror, and just move slightly to close the gap so you can't get through. Or worse still, see you coming towards them in the centre of the road because you are overtaking traffic, and either make no effort to nudge over a bit or, worse still, veer towards you. Can you believe it? This category always involves men, and always involves total bastards. Political correctness forbids me from saying what I call these people.

Ask any cyclist or motorcyclist, and I guarantee they will recognise what I am talking about. Five categories of car, van, lorry or bus drivers, self-selecting in their attitude to motorcyclists. So now ask yourself – which category do you fall into? A decent human being, an arsehole, an airhead, a fuckwit, or the latter category the soubriquet for which is the unutterable C word? There is no sixth alternative.

But now going back a bit, the reason I say that it is all so much worse today than it was when I resumed motorcycling towards the end of the last century is, of course, the mobile phone. Everyone has had their near-miss caused by an idiot yabbering away on the mobile phone. If you are on a motorbike and you see someone approaching you from the other direction and gradually veering towards your side of the road, chances are he's talking on a mobile phone. If you are overtaking traffic and someone is edging out into the middle of the road, forcing you into the path of the oncoming cars, he's always on the phone.

Then came the ban on talking on hand-held mobiles and most of us allowed ourselves to believe that things would get better. But have they? Have they hell. It's all so much worse. Why? Because now, instead of chattering away with one hand on the wheel but at least with their eyes on the road, they're texting! I guarantee it.

Every time I am ever riding my motorbike and damn nearly get hit by a car that is wandering out of its lane, when I get alongside it the bloke is looking down and sending a text. Or an email. Or looking up the cricket score on his Billberry or iPhone or whatever it is. Ten times more dangerous than when they were when they were just yabbering.

After a few years of commuting on the Kawasaki, I traded it in for a Moto-Guzzi California Special – which was entirely comfortable and looked great, but for all sorts of reasons didn't feel practical for daily use. Eventually I traded that in for a BMW 1150, which was also great until one day last year when I left the office to go home and found a large gap where I felt sure I had left the bike.

It was one of those weird things which you probably only recognise if something similar has happened to you. I found myself examining the gap where it had been as if to see if it was in there somewhere. A bit like Basil Fawlty looking for the duck in amongst the trifle, or whatever it was. Then I spent a few moments wondering whether I had left the bike somewhere else and forgotten. Then, and only then, did I realise that someone must have stolen it.

You know the rest. I spoke to the police, who said that if it had been stolen two hours earlier the chances were that already it didn't exist as a single item and that, even as we were speaking, it was being broken down for sale as spares on eBay. Apparently a BMW is worth about twice as much in individual spares as it would cost as a complete bike. Which is lovely.

It was my first claim on my own insurance for 30 years, so needless to say I got several thousand pounds less back than I paid for the bike, lost my no-claims bonus, and ended up about five grand out of pocket when buying a new one. Which is great and added immeasurably to the overall joy of life – or at least it would have done even if I hadn't already been a Grumpy.

So let me end this little section of Grumpy bile with a little story which, I promise, actually happened about three months ago on the 3-lane carriageway from the Robin Hood roundabout heading towards Wandsworth. You probably don't know it, but many people do, because it's a bottleneck on the way into London for tens of thousands of us every day. If not, try to form a mental picture.

I was on my bike and there were two bikes ahead of me, making use of the space between the cars in the two right-hand lanes. All three of us were weaving in and out and trying to get to the head of the queue. At some point we all had to stop because there was a car in the extreme right-hand lane driven by someone who was in one of the less charitable categories listed above. At this stage it was too soon to work out which.

His car was so close to the car in the middle lane that none of us could get through.

As the traffic started to move forwards, the gap between the two rows of cars began to narrow, and this was because the car on the right was veering slowly towards the centre of the road, threatening to squash, or at least significantly to compress, the bloke on the bike in front of me.

These things take only a few seconds, and there was momentary panic as the motorcyclist blasted his horn and tried to draw the attention of the driver on his right to what was happening. Still the car edged forward, and still it veered to the left, narrowing the gap still further.

Just in the nick of time, the car in front moved away, opening up a space, so that the driver of the car on the left could move forwards and allow the motorcyclist room to escape. Obviously shaken and probably a bit angry, the motorcyclist pulled in front of the car on the right, presumably with a view to remonstrating with the driver. But he couldn't – because the car had come to a halt. I looked in the window. The other motorcyclists looked in the window. The car driver was fast asleep!

By this time I was alongside, and I watched as the motorcyclist in front hammered on the bonnet of this bloke's car, trying to get his attention. Eventually the driver looked up as though suddenly awoken from a deep slumber, and even then he didn't seem to know what was going on. And this was at 8.30 in the morning, in the middle of one of the busiest commuter rush hours anywhere in the world. The driver was sound asleep! You just don't know what to say, do you? But at least I think I know which category we'll put him in to.

19 Boys' toys

Grumpiness, as those of us thus afflicted are all aware, is an all-pervasive condition. It never leaves us. It's always there, filtering our view of the world we see around us.

This does not mean that we are miserable about everything, or that we complain about everything, or that we are grouchy about everything. Not a bit of it. As I am constantly at pains to point out, Grumpies are not unhappy.

It simply means that we view every aspect of the world through our Grumpy perspective.

Where the rest of the world sees marketing, we see bullshit. Where the rest of the world sees celebrity we see self-promoting airheads. Where the rest of the world sees politicians we see ... yes, well, I guess that in the case of politicians we see the same thing everyone else sees.

From time to time I've been asked why Grumpies don't band together and form a political party themselves, and I have to admit that from time to time I have been tempted. After all, we could scarcely do a worse job of running things than the people who do so currently.

The thing that has stopped me is the realisation that while Grumpies are united by what we are against, where we are not so good is on agreeing on what we favour. As a political party we'd be great on the 'what we want to abolish' bit of the manifesto, but not so good on the 'what we propose instead ...' bit.

We all hate automated call centres, interfering bureaucracy and John McCrirrick. We all despise queuing and TV programmes which humiliate people, and self-assembly furniture. But while I can think of an endless list of things we'd unanimously agree should be wrapped up in a parcel of cowdung and barbed wire and sent in a high-powered rocket into the outer reaches of the stratosphere, I can't think of a damned thing that every single one of us would approve of. Not a single thing. And that's because in the end Grumpiness is a broad church which incorporates some right-wingers and some left-wingers and (yes you've guessed right – you could see it coming and I couldn't resist it) – some total whingers.

So, to take just a single example, I have been unable to identify a common Grumpy position either in favour or opposed to gadgets. Are we in favour of gadgets in general as a source of diversion, novelty and occasionally even fun? Or are we against them as a source of irritation, frustration and unnecessary expenditure?

It's impossible to be a bloke and remain unaware that there are a lot of us who get off on gadgets of one kind or another. We complain about computers taking over and running our lives, but then we go out and buy one and can never leave it alone. We are irritated by iPods but then many of us end up thinking how good it would be to have all your old music in one place. Loads of us resisted mobile phones for as long as possible, but it seems to me that only the real vintage and hard-core Grump has managed to resist them altogether.

But, is it just me, or is the GPS system a crock of shit?

I mention it because it seems to me that the GPS has been the toy-of-choice for so many Grumpy Old Men of my acquaintance recently, surpassing the preceding craze for iPods, MP3 players and the internet on your phone.

Everywhere I look, or have looked, for the past two years, there seem to be advertisements for little TV screens which blink away on your dashboard and provide yet another distraction to make you more likely to plough into the lollypop lady or, worse still, me when I am riding my motorcycle. As if that wasn't bad enough, I see that little GPS systems are being incorporated into your mobile phone – designed, presumably, to provide anyone under the age of 25 with essential information about how far away they are from the nearest pizza, or crack dealer, or whatever it is that interests young people these days.

For the Grumpy, I guess the clearest steer you can get about whether a gadget will excite our enthusiasm or further stimulate our ennui (if that isn't a contradiction in terms) is whether it fulfils just two simple conditions: 1) does it work? and 2) can you use it without reading the instructions?

Yes, might as well face it, we all hate reading the instructions. This is partly our fault because we are impatient bastards who don't like being told anything at all. But obviously it's much more the fault of manufacturers who insist on producing a manual the size of the Domesday Book for something designed to tell you how to turn the gas on.

And while we are on the subject, why do you suppose it is that there is an inverse relationship between the size of the device and the volume of the instructions? A tumble drier comes with a small pamphlet, a television comes with a small volume, and an MP3 player comes with the equivalent of the complete works of Trollope. Or is it Balzac? Anyway, you get the idea.

Wiser manufacturers of all things electronic have spotted this problem and tend to also produce and include among the copious packaging a 'quick set-up guide' – a single sheet so-named with no apparent sense of self-irony whatsoever. Invariably this will consist of between 8 and 14 little drawings.

First of all there will be a 'kit of parts'. The stuff you are supposed to have got in the package. So tell the truth; have you ever laid out all the bits and pieces the way they lay them out in the picture in order to ensure that everything is all present and correct? Has anyone? And anyway, how are you supposed to tell the difference between the 12 x 35mm screws and the 10 x 38mm screws?

The next pictures in the 'quick set-up guide' are supposed to illustrate the layouts of the backs of all the components, often with anything up to a dozen unidentifiable wires connecting them. Usually there will be red or green or black or yellow wires, with little jack-plugs on the end – and this is just for the microwave. Most often the pictures in the package I get relate to a model which isn't quite the model I have bought, but the manufacturers think it's sufficiently similar that I won't be confused. They are wrong. I am always confused.

And obviously it's always ideal if the instructions have been translated from the original Japanese or Norwegian by a student. Preferably of engineering.

I hold the instructions up this way, and then turn them around and hold them that way. I can never tell where the little jack-plugs are intended to go, and the holes are usually located under a little ridge so they are neatly out of sight and have to be located by touch. I never know whether this flimsy wire is optional or not. Usually, in the end I can get the thing to work after a fashion, but am always left with the sneaky feeling that it isn't working exactly as it should. Something, somewhere, hasn't been connected properly.

No, for me and other Grumpies like me, we can usually manage to put the batteries in if we have to, and we can just about plug it in if we have to, but after that we want to be able to sit back and watch it set itself up to where we live, or locate and load up whatever channels we want to receive, or whatever it is, and that's that. Anything more complicated than that and we're sunk. We get bad-tempered, and then everyone in our household has to tiptoe around for a little while. Which makes us more bad-tempered, and then we want to throw the bloody thing against the wall, and sometimes we do.

Getting back to the GPS though, in my experience this piece of kit fails on both Grumpy criteria: i.e. it doesn't really work, and the instructions are far too complicated. Put another way, it's a crock.

The first GPS I had was in a rather snazzy Range Rover which ITV gave me in 1999. I remember the date because I recall edging through a huge crowd of pedestrians who were on their way to the millennium celebrations on the Thames. God knows what persuaded me to go there. Usually this is the kind of event I'll avoid at all costs, but someone must have told me it wasn't coming around for another 100 years, so if I broke a personal rule, and agreed to go to this one, at least it wouldn't set a precedent. Obviously I wished I hadn't, but that's not the point of the story.

The point of the story is that on this occasion a group of lads, whose toes I nearly managed to drive over, were walking close enough to the side of the car to spot the little screen for the GPS on the dashboard. Obviously it was enough of a novelty at the time to get the guys' attention and make them risk more flattened toes as they strayed perilously close to my moving vehicle and one of them pointed it out.

So then the whole lot of them started jogging alongside the car for 50 yards or so to get a better look at it. I think this was so that they could admire it, or maybe it was because they wanted to take the piss. It was a while ago and I can't really remember.

I recall that for some weeks this gadget was in the mental filing cabinet listed under 'stuff I need to get around to', but in the meantime there was the nauseating voice of the American woman politely but insistently telling me to 'do a U-turn at the next exit'. I remember this being an enormous novelty in the beginning, and we ran the gamut of all the jokes you've had in your car about the various ways in which she might express running out of patience because we don't do what she is saying. Hilarious, huh?

Anyway, the novelty continued for a day or so, but then it very decidedly wore off, and I couldn't find a way to shut her the hell up.

I pressed every visible button, twiddled every available knob, placed my fingers over different touch-sensitive sensors, in different combinations, but could I find the way to switch this bloody woman off? In the end, just as my next move was to try to programme in directions for Beachy Head and leap out at the last moment, I located the volume control, which (for some reason one can only speculate on) was conveniently positioned under my seat. I managed to turn down the volume and remained content to wait for an occasion when I might need her before seeking to make her acquaintance again.

That moment eventually came one day when I was in Salisbury and unexpectedly had to make a journey to visit someone in hospital somewhere in Milton Keynes. Yes, that's right, Milton Keynes. I know it must sound as though I am making that up as a sort of ultimate challenge to the GPS system – imagine trying to find somewhere in Milton Keynes! – but honestly, it's true.

I won't go through the long laborious process of trying to instruct this machine on where I wanted to go. You've done it yourself and, if I'm honest, time and extensive treatment for post-traumatic stress disorder have filtered out most of it from my memory. Suffice it to say that I followed the instructions fairly well until I got to somewhere in the sort of Middle Wallop area, and that's when things started to go wrong.

For example, what do you do when you reach a junction, or a roundabout, and there is a bloody big sign saying 'M6 North', and all your experience, knowledge and instincts tell you that you need to be on the 'M6 North' but the sodding GPS system is telling you to take a different turning? What do you do then?

Well I know what I do now, but this was my first experience of this supposed magical machine and I remember thinking something along the lines of – 'oh well, maybe that's the point. This little machine is much cleverer than the rest of us, and has worked out an unknown but much better route.' I think I even remember enjoying the anticipation of being able to gloat that I had arrived by entirely unexpected roads, half an hour before the predicted time, just because of my ownership and mastery of a very clever gadget.

Is anyone still thinking that that's what happened?

For some reason best known to myself, I decided to follow this machine slavishly. Even though it started to tell me things which frankly felt ever-more unlikely, I remember thinking, 'No, this thing must know much better than me. Let's follow it.'

However, after a while, the instructions emanating from this little gadget were so counter-intuitive that I had no clear idea where the hell I was, and so my ordinary powers of intuit were no longer functioning anyway. I had no choice but to follow the increasingly eccentric orders being issued by this damned machine – up to and including at one point darting around the back of a row of terraced houses, along a lane which was obviously mostly used for accessing their garages – and back out into the street I had turned off. I'd say it was just like a scene from *The Italian Job*, except that I've already said that somewhere else. So I won't.

Well, I think you can probably guess what had happened, but I of course had no idea about any pre-set instructions that you are supposed to impart to the machine during 'set up'. And of course I had no idea that the sodding thing was set to 'shortest route' and 'avoiding A-roads'. So I think that a journey, which shouldn't have taken more than three hours took closer to five, and boy was I hacked off when I got there. Needless to say, I didn't spend too much time showing off about the new gadget.

Even having had the need to set this thing up in the desired 'mode' pointed out to me, variations on the same adventure have happened to me quite a few times since, and I guess they have happened to you. But after a while I got the hang of it, and from time to time have found the machine fairly useful. Especially when trying to navigate my way around what seems to be an endless maze of roundabouts through and around Milton Keynes. Have you ever done that? Blimey.

However, what is still fairly disconcerting is what happens when for some reason you set the GPS to choose the best route for a journey you know like the back of your hand, and you find that it picks a different one. That's undermining, isn't it? When that happens, I find that any goodwill that the machine may have drawn to itself over several weeks all goes out the window in an instant.

For example, I frequently make a journey from my house in Kingston to the same place in the New Forest. I've done this

journey about 500 times and, believe me, I have tried every variation of the route, short of going via Belgium. The shortest distance I have ever been able to travel is 88 miles, but have I ever been able to persuade the GPS to find a route of less than 95? Even on the 'shortest' regulo? No I haven't, and so any faith I may have entrusted in the thing has taken a knock, to the extent that these days I never rely on it unless I am absolutely clueless as to where something is, and then I'll use it with more optimism than faith, and with the map in one hand and the steering wheel in the other.

Like most of us, I eventually got the hang of the thing, and have had them in several different cars since. My last GPS used to like me to enter the name of the town or city, which I usually knew, then the street, which I also usually knew. All this worked relatively well. However, that's obviously far too simple and straightforward for the latest one, which seems to like to be programmed by first putting in the postcode.

Frequently, of course, you don't know the postcode for the place you want to go to. What is the postcode for your local pub, for example? No, I thought not. But even if you do know it, this thing won't let you enter more than 4 letters and digits. So I can't put in SP6 2EJ, because after I have entered SP6 2, it won't register any more digits, but instead wants to know the street name. But even if I know the street name I am not allowed to just enter it – this machine wants to show me a selection of street names which it believes are in that postcode and have me choose one. The trouble is that on many occasions, even when I know for certain that a particular street name exists in that particular postcode, it doesn't show up on the list of streets this thing has listed. And there is no plan B. So at this point I am stuffed.

Or is it that I haven't read the instructions properly?

Recently I bought a second-hand Mercedes, the first owner of which had specified all sorts of exciting gadgets, with the result that I now have an even more super-duper coked-up GPS which incorporates a whiz-bang way of predicting what the traffic will be like.

I first got to know about this facility when sitting in a five-mile traffic jam and glancing down at the GPS, to see the little arrow that indicates where I am, crowded in on all sides by long lines of little red lights going one way and little yellow lights going the other way. At the front of this row of little red lights was a tiny, weeny version of the symbol I recognise as meaning 'road works', beyond which the road ahead seemed to once again be clear.

Consumed by curiosity, and anyway with ten minutes to spare before the car could move again, I reached for the instruction booklet, which had remained untouched in the glove box, and flicked through the pages until I saw a picture of the screen with lots of red and yellow lights on it. So apparently this thing knows when there are road works under way, and also receives signals from sensors indicating high density of traffic. Cool!

I thought this was devilishly clever and for several months, when planning or under way on a journey, I started to search ahead a little way on my screen to see if I could anticipate a hold-up. Quite frequently I did indeed see such a hold-up, and so whenever I could detect a little cluster of red lights on the road ahead of me, I would take a sometimes huge detour to avoid them. Often this detour would take me many miles out of my way, and add maybe half an hour to my journey time, but still I had the smug satisfaction of knowing that I would otherwise have been caught in a long traffic queue.

Schadenfreude is an especially unattractive emotion, but I probably should admit to feeling just a hint of it when contemplating all those suckers sitting in the traffic jam from which 21st-century technology had set me free.

That was all very fine and for about three months I thought this was an absolutely brilliant wheeze. Then a couple of times I found myself flying down long stretches of carriageway with hardly another car in sight, and glancing down at the GPS screen and seeing my virtual self surrounded on all sides by little red and yellow lights indicating appalling hold-ups and traffic jams. Gridlock on the screen, and hardly a car in sight on the road around me.

Or is that because I haven't properly read the instructions? Anyway, it doesn't matter because now of course I ignore the thing. Altogether.

20 Top Gear

Are you getting a bit fed up with *Top Gear*?

I feel a bit uncomfortable even to ask the question because Jeremy Clarkson is one of our favourite Grumpy Old Men from the TV series, and has flown the flag in just about everything he has done since. You name it, he's Grumpy about it – definitely one of us.

As a matter of fact what actually happened was that we asked Jeremy to be in the first TV series, but at the time he turned us down because he was too busy, and anyway was no doubt irritated with being asked to contribute to all those dreadful celebrity vox-pop shows which used to drive us all crazy. We then heard later that he couldn't watch *Grumpy Old Men* after episode 2 because he was so upset not to have been in it. So he appeared in series 2 and in the special we made about Christmas. He was great. The real McCoy – whoever that is.

I don't want to be name-dropping or sound too much of a creep, but we also like Richard Hammond, with whom we did some work a couple of years ago. Charming bloke, really good fun, excellent. I don't know James May but he seems to be a decent enough cove. Bit of a dodgy haircut, but let's not worry too much about that. Some of us have problems of our own in that area.

So it's only with some reluctance that we even posit the question. Are we getting a bit fed up with *Top Gear*?

Like everyone else, I was glad when the programme stopped being about cars. In the early years it had been very much a series for people I believe are known by the curiously unappealing term 'petrolheads'. Since most petrolheads are probably out in the evenings, burning up the rubber or the tarmac or whatever it is that petrolheads do, the show had a fairly limited audience. It did OK, for a show about cars, but only OK.

Then one day some bright spark worked out that the series shouldn't really be about cars at all. It should be about three unreconstructed 'blokes' enjoying themselves, and so that's what it turned into, and it has been terrific.

What a laugh these geezers have had at the licence-payers' expense. One of my favourite items involved propelling a series of cars off a cliff and into a quarry, in which someone had painted a dartboard. Playing darts with cars – why didn't we think of that? Another was an elaborate set-up enabling the three to play conkers with caravans. Why? Because Jeremy doesn't really like caravans. How many of us would love to be able to do that? Take something we don't like and hurl it skywards into a ravine. And get paid for it. Wow!

I remember another one which involved seeing how much damage they could do to a Toyota pick-up truck before it would cease to run. You know, those beasts you see all over Africa or anywhere else where neglect and abuse are likely to be the norm. Usually with half a dozen 16-year-olds hanging off the back wearing Manchester United shirts and carrying a Kalashnikov. Eventually I think they dropped this truck off a cliff and, after a tiny intervention from a mechanic, the engine still started. A gas.

But the reason why this show ultimately has to be about big kids having fun is that, let's face it, cars as such are a bit boring. Yes they are. Cars are a bit boring because it is the first decade of the 21st century, and we've more or less cracked it. It's the 'noughties' – a word with which I may get on familiar terms by the time the decade is nearly over but not before – it's the 'noughties' and all cars are more or less the same. The fact is that, with very few exceptions, all cars are excellent.

These days there is hardly such a thing as a bad car; which may sound like something we should all be grateful for, but if you are a Grumpy and tend to see the negative in everything, it seems to have taken away some of the welcome colour and variety of life.

In the old days there was a whole range of very important critical things you could say about cars, and a lot of important and interesting comparisons to be made about them. Vauxhalls used to look OK but were legendary rust-buckets. Jaguars went through a phase of being very smart but very unreliable. Peugeots were crap, are crap, and always will be crap. Citroëns were stylish but tinny. Austins had terrible design (you doubt it? think Austin Princess. Think Austin Maestro). Volvos were solid but sluggish etc, etc, etc. I'll bet you could add some more smears of one kind or another – no doubt some of them more fair than others, but the kind of generalised prejudice we Grumpies thrive on.

Time was when there were also comparisons to be made in terms of important things such as reliability. These were the days when any longish trip involved seeing any number of cars stuck at the side of the road, their bonnets thrown open and steam billowing out from an overheated or leaky radiator. Poor sod in a sweat, scratching his head, the family looking hapless and abandoned on the side of the road, the kids wanting to complain but knowing that to do so would earn them a thick ear.

Or you'd occasionally see a car bombing down the road, spewing out black smoke like a burning rainforest because a piston ring in the engine had split. And how often would you hear a blown exhaust pipe?

Nowadays you seldom if ever see any of the above, and the reason is that all cars do essentially the same thing, very well indeed. You can buy a brand-new car for about £5,000 which is every bit as reliable, maybe more so, than the car you will pay £50,000 for, or £500,000 for. And on most journeys it'll get you there in the same time.

They all have great road holding, smart clear instrument panels, ergonomically designed seats (whatever that means), air bags, extended service intervals and long guarantees. And the truth is, they are all much of a muchness. All more or less the same.

All credit to Jeremy, Richard and James for continually putting all manner of new cars through their paces, inventing new ways to compare this with that, and for interminably finding new excuses to throw this one round lots of corners, or to lob that one off the side of a mountain to see whether or not it bounces. (It doesn't.) But really ...

No ... *Top Gear* ... so much better since it stopped being about cars ... but how many more big boys' pranks can they come up with before we get bored out of our trees? Well I guess we'll see.

21 Road rage

When you hear a siren in the distance, which seems to be approaching you rapidly, do you always know which direction it's coming from?

I only ask because it seems to me that at one time I always did, and now it seems to me that frequently I don't.

Of course when Grumpies were little, the police, fire and ambulance services used to announce their approach with a nice bell. A shiny stainless-steel thing bolted smartly on the front of their vehicles, which rang loud enough to wake the dead and seemed to me to do a very effective job of alerting people to their approach. Indeed, if turned on unexpectedly and at close quarters, there was an imminent risk among the elderly of an involuntary evacuation of the bowels. These were the days, of course, before it was usual to pelt ambulance men with bricks, or fire pellet guns at firemen when they arrive at the scene of the arson. Yes, it was well before then.

As you might predict, as someone of a Grumpy persuasion I rather preferred the bell to the siren. There was something

very British about it. It heralded in our minds all those images
of firemen dropping into their trousers like something out of
Wallace and Gromit, and then spiralling down long poles on
their way to put out the blaze in a chip-pan. Or to rescue a cat
from a tree. Very British stuff I think. The only times we ever
heard sirens in those days was in films featuring American
cops or equally recent newsreels about the Blitz.

So anyway, at some point the emergency services started
replacing bells with sirens. I'm guessing that perhaps some
smart alec somewhere probably argued that the sound waves
involved in the siren lend themselves better to what I believe
is known as the Doppler effect, which at least better enables
you to determine whether a sound is coming towards you or
going away from you. Possible. More probably it was a police
chief somewhere preferring the image of Starsky and Hutch
to that of Dixon of Dock Green, and a whole aspect of our way
of life went down the Swanee.

However, speak as you find I always say, and what I find
is that I cannot always tell from which direction they are
approaching. I might be stopped at the traffic lights, I hear the
wail of a distant siren, and cannot immediately identify whether
it's coming from in front of me, from behind me, from the left
or from the right. Therefore I don't instantly know what is the
best option for getting out of the way, and so then I end up as
one of those total jerks I've spent most of my life taking the
piss out of because they're evidently thrown into a panic by an
oncoming panda car.

Which is great. And adds immeasurably to my Grumpiness.

I suppose we should be grateful that, by and large, it still
seems to be the general instinct to try to make way for
emergency vehicles. One can only imagine that a natural

development of our fast deteriorating social consideration is that eventually we won't bother. 'So someone is ill or injured; or someplace is on fire. So what? It's probably not me. Fuck it.'

However, that's for the not too distant future. For the moment, you have only to witness the mayhem on any congested dual carriageway as people try to work out whether to pull onto the kerb, or to speed out of the way, or to jump the traffic lights or mow down the pedestrian.

Which reminds me of a question I've frequently asked myself in these situations. If an ambulance speeding to the scene of an accident knocks you over, does he stop and pick you up in preference to hurrying on to the accident he was going to? Or does he continue on his route and call another one to come to collect you? Have you wondered about this?

I only ask because, as we all know, nowadays there are of course targets for everything, including ambulance response times. So if they hurry on to the original destination and call another ambulance for you, they've probably got a chance of reaching both within their target time limits. If on the other hand they stop and attend to you in preference to the other person, they'll beat their target response time for you, but miss it for the original bloke. Does anyone else torture themselves with all this bollocks? God I hope so.

Anyway, back to getting out of the way of the emergency vehicle blasting their siren in your ear-hole. As often as not, the evasive action you see drivers taking is more likely to cause a hold-up than to let the speeding police car through. There are no hard and fast rules for quite how to do this and, if you are the kind of driver who just drives by the rules and has no real instincts for it, you're almost certain, in your panic, to do the wrong thing.

When that happens, all the rest of us who are stuck behind and can't get out of the way because this other person didn't get out of the way, go into our own little individual ritual of cursing and swearing – whatever is your family variation of 'what a bloody idiot – why doesn't he pull over to the right rather than just coming to a dead halt in the middle of the bus lane?' I guess we've all got our own version of that.

Being a Grumpy, and therefore fancying myself a reasonably decent driver in most circumstances, on the occasions when I can just tell where the sodding thing is coming from, I usually know how most effectively to get out of the way. And to be fair, so do most other people. But exactly how annoying is it when you have pulled off the road to allow an emergency vehicle past you, and you find that the other cars behind you try to take the opportunity to jump the queue of traffic?

You know the sort of thing. You've pulled into the side of the road, and the car behind you has pulled into the side of the road, but as the fire engine passes by, he is free to pull back out again before you are free to pull out. So he wants to overtake you.

How annoying is that?

Worse still is the driver who thinks it's very clever to try to tuck in behind the emergency vehicle, speeding along in its wake, and thereby quite literally pulling a fast one on all the rest of the traffic. This sort of thing is the reason for gun-control laws. There is a strong argument, I think, that behaviour like this should be punishable by instant execution, administered by any concerned citizen witnessing the scene.

Which of course would have a better chance of being funny if it wasn't also sometimes true. Another thing that came from America, along with sirens, is the now familiar term 'road rage'.

When did you first hear the expression 'road rage'? I don't know if this is just me but I have a feeling that it's not an expression we ever heard as kids, and that road rage is just another of those wonderful phenomena which goes with modern living.

Obviously I'm not saying that no-one on the roads lost their tempers when we were little. Sure they did. If I delve into my childhood memory I can easily put together a mental montage of altercations ranging from people raising their eyeballs, as if to search the inside of their frontal lobes for an answer to the slow-wittedness of a woman driver in front of them, all the way to a bloke in Brixton High Street winding down his window and suggesting to a taxi driver that he might benefit from taking an eye-test. 'You want your head examined' was about as bad as it got, sometimes accompanied by the abuser pointing an index finger at his own temple and winding it slowly in a circle to indicate 'you're mental'. Serious stuff.

I can certainly recall the odd blast on a car horn lasting one to two seconds, and I'm not even sure that I didn't once see a bloke get out of his car in a ten-minute traffic jam over the Hog's Back and complain to the people stuck alongside him that 'the place is going to rack and ruin' – another expression I've never quite understood, but that's by the by.

In all honesty, I don't think I can remember any traffic-induced temper tantrums which were very much more than that as a kid. Naturally all this got worse as our social mores deteriorated over the years, but not too much worse.

Instinctively preferring prejudice to evidence, Grumpies don't actually research things like this, but it seems as though an American journalist called Michael Fumento has done the work.

Fumento claims that the term 'road rage' was first coined

in a newspaper in the US in 1988, that it appeared in up to three stories a year until 1994 when it received 27 mentions, and then spread from there. In 1995, according to this bloke, the term 'road rage' appeared in US publications almost 500 times. In 1996 the phrase appeared over 1,800 times, and in 1997 there were over 4,000 usages of the term in the popular media.

Nowadays road rage is such a commonplace occurrence in America that no-one dares to provoke anyone else, or to respond to provocation, because there is a very reasonable chance that the little old lady in a 'Driving Miss Daisy' hat will pull out a Magnum (and I don't mean a chocolate lolly on a stick) and blow your bloody head off.

So first of all we read about these incidents in America

and then, like everything bad, at some point it is imported over here. I can't honestly say that I remember the precise incident, but I do recall being shocked at the first time I heard that someone had been stabbed in a dispute between drivers. It was one of those 'what is the world coming to?' moments that all of us seem to enjoy so perversely, and that we Grumpies consider to be yet further confirmation that it's all going to hell.

Until the development of road rage it was generally part of our God-given right to shout a bit of generalised abuse at another driver. Anything from a gentle shake of the head in disbelief at one extreme, to the full on, leaning out of the window, making huge gestures indicating masturbation, and inviting the other driver to perform a sexual activity only available to especially agile transsexuals.

Not especially charming, I am sure you will agree, but all part of the birthright of the British. A bit of letting off steam, no doubt unpleasant, but essentially harmless.

Not any more. These days no-one in their right mind would remonstrate with another driver, no matter how idiotic their behaviour, and no matter how apparently meek and mild-mannered they may seem. Oh no sirree.

These days there is always the possibility that the apparently meek and mild-mannered bloke in the car next to you is on his way to climb to the top of a tower and unleash his Uzi on the unsuspecting students walking underneath. Or the apparent burk has stashed a machete under his seat and is just waiting for the next person to call him a spotty-faced dweeb to wreak the vengeance of an old-testament God on his accuser. Or the little lady who has put up with torment from an abusive husband for 20 years and has chosen today to cut off his gonads while he is sleeping and so both the gonads and the kitchen carving knife are in the same plastic shopping bag under her seat.

A little far-fetched? Well maybe, but these days who is willing to take the chance? A bloke walks out into the street and asks three 12-year-olds not to slash his tyres, and has his throat cut for his trouble. A next-door neighbour asks if the football can come over the garden wall just a little less frequently and is kicked to death for his disrespect.

Oh no; it's a whole new world out there and those of us of a sensitive disposition have entirely abandoned the idea of giving expression to any element of displeasure at the behaviour of our fellow-citizens. It's the 21st century and psychopaths rule the streets. Some of them would kill you as soon as look at you. Sooner.

And if that simple fact alone isn't enough to explain to non-Grumpies why Grumpies are grumpy, then it's hard to see what would be.

22 A little diversion

For the whole of this volume so far I have been trying to find the right place to include one of my favourite car-related stories. However, we are now nearly at the end and I haven't found the right place, so I've just said bugger it, let's give it a little chapter of its own. Otherwise there is a danger that it might get left out of this otherwise comprehensive tome.

The story goes back a very long time to when I got my first job in the BBC, and for a brief period was attached to the TV bulletins on BBC2. My boss at the time was a delightful bloke from New Zealand called Dick Ross. Dick was a larger-than-life, highly entertaining fellow, with a great range of personal anecdotes. One of them appealed to me so much that I've remembered it over the years, and may occasionally even have been guilty of retelling it as though it had happened to me. Do you do that? I sometimes do. Actually some of these stories I've told so often that I can't remember whether they happened to me or not, but that's another matter.

Last I heard of Dick was about 1975 when I believe he was

returning to New Zealand – so Dick, if by any chance you are reading this, feel free to contact me and claim your £5.

It seems that Dick was invited on holiday to a house somewhere in France, which a friend of his was renovating. Part of the deal for people staying there was that you had to undertake a little task – to make a contribution to the various renovations and improvements being carried out to the place. Dick's task was to help to dig out a whole heap of rubble that had been accumulating in the swimming pool. However, he wasn't required to do this alone. He had the help of a French friend who also, handily, owned an ancient sort of pick-up truck, which could be used to transport the rubble to the local tip.

It seems that they had piled on board the first load of rubble and were on their way to the dump, which was maybe ten kilometres away. It was only at this point that Dick realised that this was a very old vehicle indeed, that there was a hole on the floor of the van at his feet, and that through the hole he could see the speeding blur of the gravel road they were passing over.

He didn't think much more about it until a couple of kilometres later when he thought that maybe he could smell burning. He looked around and thought that he could also see a little bit of smoke. He then glanced down and, through the hole in the floor, he could see sparks flying from something apparently scraping on the road.

Somewhat alarmed, he noisily drew this to the attention of his friend, the Frenchman, who was preoccupied in driving the car and told Dick that he need not be concerned.

Dick didn't find it too easy to be unconcerned, but he did his best, assuming that this phenomenon must be a common one for his French compatriot. However, after a few minutes more he glanced down again, only to see that the flying sparks had now begun to join up, and were providing a continuous flame which seemed to be being fanned by the wind.

Once again, and now with rather more alarm, Dick sought to draw the attention of the driver to this problem. Bordering on being irritated by his over-anxious English passenger, the Frenchman glanced over, looked down, peered into the hole and immediately began to shout. 'Mon Dieu' he is reported to have said (though frankly I wouldn't have much faith in this particular detail). 'Mon Dieu – we are on fire!'

With that the Frenchman jerked the vehicle to the side of the road, slammed on the brakes, leapt out onto the pavement and then immediately up on to the bonnet, whereupon he whipped open his flies and proceeded to piss with stunning accuracy directly onto the seat of the flames. The result was a huge hissing noise, large volumes of smoke, and a stench so acrid that Dick was instantly close to throwing up on the spot.

However, this obviously much practised safety technique did the trick and, all at once, Dick felt so relieved by his narrow escape that he got out of the van, stumbled across to the side of the road, and proceeded to take a leak himself. At this point he felt the full force of the Frenchman belabouring him around the head and neck with his fists and shouting the words, 'What are you doing? What are you doing?' Dick had no choice but to interrupt himself mid flow and asked what was the problem.

'What is the problem? What is the problem?' asked the excitable Frenchman. 'We have 12 kilometres to go, and you are the reserve fire extinguisher!'

23 Torturing the metaphor

Longer term students of the Grumpy syndrome are well used to our unendearing habit of torturing innocent metaphors until they scream for mercy. It's not something we're proud of. We don't think it's funny or clever. It's just something we do.

So you won't be surprised, I hope, to learn that our theme provides just such an opportunity, which we find to be far too tempting to be resisted. Indeed, it throws wide open all its limbs in a proffered embrace which is so seductive that, in my book at least, we are powerless to do anything other than take the plunge.

Ready? Take a deep breath and follow me.

One of the reasons why Grumpy Old Men and Grumpy Old Women are grumpy when we think about motoring is that driving cars over a long journey provides an all too vivid and immediate allegory of our lives. And so exploring this little allegory, just briefly, may help to explain the reasons why we are so hacked off.

When we all started out, the car was new, the road seemed

open, the journey seemed never ending; we felt on the brink of an adventure that would take an eternity. We just couldn't wait to get started.

All around us there were those who had done the journey before and wanted to give us their bits of advice on how to keep out of scrapes. But we weren't really interested in other people's maps or directions; after all this was our trip and we wanted to do it our way. We didn't listen carefully enough.

We had enormous confidence at the start that we knew where we wanted to get to and the direction we were heading to get there. We set off at breakneck speed, seldom stopping to check where we were going or to look around ourselves. Inevitably it wasn't all that long before we found that it might have been a good idea to glance at the map after all. Quite often we came to a junction and didn't know which route to take, but the people we should have listened to before we set off were by now just distant voices. Or maybe we could see them shouting advice, but couldn't quite hear them above the noise.

We decided to go one way, and maybe that was fine, but we couldn't help but occasionally look over our shoulder and wonder what might have been if we had taken the other.

If we were very lucky, our mistakes amounted to not much more than the odd crunch of the gears or a tyre scuffed against a high kerb. A small price to pay for experience.

If we were just a bit less lucky we got into some minor scrapes but did very little damage to ourselves or to others. Probably we more or less got away with it.

Or maybe we didn't. Maybe, just as we thought we were getting the hang of it, we got involved in a crash of some sort. People got hurt, possibly us, possibly some others. Some of the damage could be repaired, some of it could not, and some had to be written off and come to terms with. Some of it we never quite recovered from.

A bit bruised and battered perhaps, we often found that lots of other people wanted to go the same route as we were taking, but to reach where they wanted to get to they had to cut across in front of us. Often they did, causing us to veer from our paths. Sometimes maybe we cut across them, causing them to veer away from theirs. We didn't feel all that proud of ourselves, but we got ahead in any case. We shouted and raved, and they shouted and raved back. After all, we were in a race, weren't we?

Once or twice we realised in time that we were heading in the wrong direction. A quick U-turn or a bit of a diversion, and back along the better road. Not too late to change our journey mid-way. Maybe we wasted a lot of time, but most certainly we picked up a lot of useful experience in the process.

Are you still following? Lost the will to live? Don't worry: it's all downhill from here.

Because now, for some of us Grumpies, just as we reckon we are beginning to get the hang of the journey, just as we are feeling comfortable behind the wheel and have got the measure of the car, suddenly we think we can see the end in sight. What seemed just a short time ago to be a journey without end, now seems to be going by all too quickly.

There's a lot of haze on the horizon and, as we peer into it, we can't quite tell whether the end is near or far. What we know is that we've broken the back of the journey, and maybe if we're lucky we can coast for a bit before the finishing line. Maybe.

And while we're coasting, we've got time to wonder whether all the 'hurry, hurry, hurry' that seemed so essential to our journey thus far was such a good idea after all. Perhaps we were too focused on the road ahead to properly take on board everything that was going on out of the side windows? Maybe we missed a lot along the way, and that stopping from time to time to explore the countryside might have made for a more pleasant journey. And now probably it's too late. Too late to go back to some of those junctions and try another route. As the Danish philosopher Soren Kierkegaard said, 'Life can only be understood backwards, but it must be lived forwards.'

Yes that's right. Just when we're getting the hang of it, it feels like we're getting towards the end of it. It doesn't make us angry – anger is for young men and these days we reserve our anger for the bigger things. It doesn't make us sad – not yet anyway; maybe a bit later on, but not quite yet. But it does make us Grumpy. Yes that's right. We're Grumpy. Grumpy Old Men and Grumpy Old Women.

So anyway, I did say that if the metaphor was tortured it would at least be brief. And it has been. Mercifully.

24 And so, at last …

So there we are. We're nearing the end of yet another Grumpy old rant about yet another aspect of our Grumpy old lives which most people just regard as commonplace and everyday, and which Grumpies regard as a source of vexation.

Let's face it, driving is just a more or less unavoidable part of living in the 21st century. So why, I can hear some people ask, make an issue of it? Why not, in the time-honoured and almost incredibly irritating expression, 'grin and bear it'?

Well we could do that. 'Grinning and bearing it' is an option. There is even an argument that instead of identifying, pointing out and making an enormous fuss about driving and other related and unrelated irritations which dog us from dawn 'til dusk, we might be more cheerful if we decided to 'grin and bear it'.

But that, I am afraid, is to miss the point entirely. And it's an important point to miss, so let's take a few seconds before we close to see if we can nail it.

When various volumes of the Grumpy books have been published, I usually find myself doing the rounds of local radio stations to do a bit of promotion. This I find is almost always enjoyable, and it is especially generous of the producers and presenters to have me back insofar as, from time to time, I have been less than complimentary about some of their output. In the vast majority of cases the host completely 'gets it', often indeed is 'one of us', and we have a lot of fun comparing notes on what makes them Grumpy versus what makes me Grumpy. Usually we have quite a lot in common.

However, there is a female presenter on one BBC local radio station who always wants to give me a little bit of a hard time. She doesn't mean anything by it, I don't think, but she just can't stop herself. She always feels the need to ask me something like 'don't Grumpy Old Men and Grumpy Old Women just make us all miserable by drawing attention to the negative in everything?'

See what I mean? Irritating in itself, but she is a really nice woman, obviously a very cheerful soul who enjoys bringing sunshine into the lives of her listeners, colleagues and those around her. So usually I attempt to fend this off with good grace and we have a laugh before we get to the end of the interview. I don't know what she says about me once I'm off the air; but at the time it all seems relatively good humoured.

The last time this happened, though, she was going on and on and on about how Grumpy people would be better off 'looking on the bright side' and that our constant complaining made the world a more depressing place, and you can probably see why eventually this started to get on my nerves.

'Wouldn't it be so much better', she twittered, 'if Grumpy people could just look out for what is nice about the world instead of always going on about what's wrong with it? Wouldn't they make themselves a whole lot happier if they did?'